A Sourcebook For Literacy Work

Perspective from the
Grassroots
H.S. Bhola

Jessica Kingsley Publishers/UNESCO Publishing

Published by UNESCO and the UNESCO Institute for Education with a contribution from the German Foundation for International Development.

First published in the United Kingdom in 1994 by

Jessica Kingsley Publishers Ltd
116 Pentonville Road
London N1 9JB, England
and
1900 Frost Road, Suite 101
Bristol, PA 19007, U S A

and

The United Nations Educational,
Scientific and Cultural Organization,
7 Place de Fontenoy,
75352 Paris 07 SP

ISBN 185302

ISBN 92-3-102793-X

Library of Congress Cataloging in Publication Data

A CIP catalogue record for this book is available from the Library of Congress

British Library Cataloguing in Publication Data

A CIP catalogue record for this book is available from the British Library

Printed by The Cromwell Press, Melksham, Wiltshire

CONTENTS

Preface

As part of its continuing efforts to support literacy activities throughout the world, UNESCO decided in 1991 to prepare a practical guide to functional literacy work at grassroots level. The preparation of the guide was entrusted to Professor H. S. Bhola of Indiana University. Professor Bhola has been actively involved in literacy for many years and has published several books and articles on various aspects of literacy. He has supervised and trained a vast number of literacy and adult education students at Indiana University. He is author of *Campaigning for Literacy*, published by UNESCO in 1984.

The book addresses a range of issues that literacy workers in the field encounter almost every day: mobilizing, planning, teaching, supervising, evaluating and so on. It does not lay down hard and fast rules; instead, it reports particular situations and proposes options within a flexible framework that can be adapted to various situations in different parts of the globe.

It has been published at a very important juncture in the history of organized literacy work when specialists and policy-makers are looking for effective tools to advance the march of humanity towards a literate world. This book is certainly going to be one of those tools.

Professor Bhola is responsible for the choice and presentation of the facts contained in this book and for the opinions expressed therein, which are not necessarily those of UNESCO and do not commit the Organization.

Introduction

In development and education, grassroots work means work at the field level. It means working with the poor and the weak. It means giving them a voice and power over their own lives. It is difficult work that requires commitment and sacrifice. As a literacy worker you should be proud to be working at the grassroots. Extension workers in agriculture, health, nutrition and family planning are some others working with you at the grassroots.

Literacy workers at the grassroots are often praised but seldom well rewarded. Honoraria given to them are inadequate. Little is invested in them in other ways. Their initial training is short and in-service training rarely follows. Training materials such as teachers' guides and training manuals – when available – have not been written from their special perspective, nor in the language which they can understand. There are no opportunities for them to come together in groups to discuss common interests and concerns. They feel abandoned and helpless.

To improve matters, several initiatives need to be undertaken. We take an initiative in the area of training materials by offering *A Sourcebook for Literacy Work: Perspective from the Grassroots*.

OBJECTIVES OF THE SOURCEBOOK

The objectives of the *Sourcebook* are to answer questions such as the following: What is literacy? What is 'functional' literacy? How does literacy help farmers, workers and home makers? Does literacy bring socio-economic development? What is literacy work like at the grassroots? How is it done? What is special about workers at the grassroots level? We will answer these questions from the perspective of the literacy worker in the field. Both the question 'what' and the question 'why' will be answered.

Therein, however, lies a problem. It is easy perhaps to write training materials addressed to grassroots workers in one particular literacy project and written in one particular local or regional language understood by them. But once one wishes to address literacy workers in many different projects, working with many different languages of literacy, in many different social contexts, in far-flung countries, then the problem of writing a single sourcebook for all workers becomes a difficult challenge. It is necessary to be quite general, and thereby somewhat theoretical.

Such are the realities of field work in most of the Third World today that books written at a general level and in an international language become inaccessible to workers at the grassroots in various countries. Such books should, first, be translated in appropriate local or regional languages and, second, be mediated by a professional trainer. What we mean by mediation is that literacy workers at the grassroots should be provided with guidance in using such a sourcebook in relation to concrete problems of their own learners in their own communities. We recommend both these strategies and will have more to say about this later.

A BOOK ABOUT ALL LITERACIES

Today, people like to talk about many literacies rather than one literacy. There is talk of cultural literacy, workplace literacy, environmental literacy and much else. What was earlier referred to as teaching of reading to children is now called 'school literacy'. Literacy taught to adults in special classes and night schools is referred to as 'adult literacy'.

One of the forms of adult literacy is called 'functional literacy'. Of course, literacy always comes to find a 'function' in the lives of people who become literate. In that sense all literacy is 'functional'. However, it so happens that the phrase 'functional literacy' has acquired special meanings. A functional literacy programme is a special kind of a literacy programme for adults. In such a programme, the teaching of literacy is combined with the teaching of 'economic skills'. In functional literacy, the economic function is given a central importance. This *Sourcebook* is relevant to all kinds of literacy work with adults and to all types of literacy organizations – projects, programmes and campaigns.

COVERING MOST SETTINGS OF LITERACY WORK

Some 98 per cent of all illiterate people in the world live in the Third World, that is, in developing countries. Populations of developing countries are typically more rural than urban. Therefore, in this *Sourcebook* you will find more examples from literacy programmes in rural areas than in urban areas. However, our interests are wide. We visualize our teachers working in many settings. We see them working in rural and urban areas, on farms and factory floors. We see them working in the developing countries and in the developed world. We see them working for the government and with non-governmental organizations. We see them working on different kinds of literacy programmes. In our mind's eye, we can see literacy workers working with many different learners – men and women, farmers and workers, tribals and refugees. We also visualize very young boys and girls in some of the so-called 'adult' literacy classes. This will happen where there are no primary schools in the vicinity of villages and townships.

MANY TOPICS, MANY PERSPECTIVES

This *Sourcebook* is fairly big in size and scope. It covers the whole range of literacy topics. The emphasis is, of course, on literacy work at the grassroots. But it also covers literacy planning, programme implementation and literacy evaluation as seen from the perspective of the field-level worker.

This *Sourcebook* combines the perspective of the field worker with some other perspectives. That is, the perspective of the literacy supervisor is also covered. The interests of literacy organizers and literacy specialists are addressed as well – sometimes directly and sometimes indirectly.

Even though, the focus is on practice, the question 'Why?' is never neglected. We do not only instruct, but we also explain. To make the *Sourcebook* really practical, at least three things were kept in mind in the course of its writing:

(1) The book responds to the questions and concerns frequently expressed by literacy teachers in the field. Indeed, we have tried to look at literacy work through the eyes of a literacy teacher in the field.

(2) In every case, we have discussed the question 'Why?' When specific practical suggestions are made or a set of instructions are included, these are not meant to be followed blindly. Readers should make the best possible choices in the special context of their work in the field.

(3) Finally, we have tried to express our ideas in simple language.

The book is addressed to literacy workers within the primary (or what could be called 'official') boundaries of literacy systems. But in this book, we are also talking to people outside the primary literacy system who are making important contributions to literacy work. We are talking to teachers in elementary, middle and secondary schools. We are also talking to professors and researchers in universities.

Most important, we are talking to all extension workers at the field level. These extension workers include workers from all development ministries and development departments – agriculture, health, labour, social work, family planning and all others – because literacy can be a deciding factor in each of these endeavours.

SEMI-PROGRAMMED FORMAT

All of the above makes the *Sourcebook* a relatively complex work. We have indeed done our best to make the book manageable, usable and accessible, breaking the material down into many useful parts, and organizing these parts in a clear and obvious manner.

A list of section themes is included at the beginning of each chapter. Each chapter and each section within a chapter is self-contained and can be read more or less independently. We hope that readers will find the *Sourcebook* easy to use effectively.

HOW TO USE THE *SOURCEBOOK*

You, the reader, may have noticed already that the book's language is simple and sentences are relatively short. But then it is after all a technical book. Theories of teaching and learning can not be avoided. Concepts of planning and evaluation can not be excluded from our discussion. Although the language of the *Sourcebook* is simple, there are limits to being simple. New ideas often need new words to be fully expressed. Some literacy workers may not be familiar with these new words. Wherever possible, these new words are explained in the text itself. But these may still prove difficult for some readers. Our experience suggests that readers will need assistance in the use of this book.

AN EXPERIENCE FROM EAST AFRICA

During the 1960s, I worked as a training and methodology specialist in the United Republic of Tanzania. I was on a joint project of the Government of the United Republic of Tanzania and UNESCO. The project was called Experimental World Literacy Programme.

While there, I helped in starting a newsletter for literacy teachers who were teaching literacy within our project. We thought that pre-service training for our literacy teachers was not enough. We decided that our literacy teachers should get continuous on-the-job training. The newsletter was considered to be a good solution.

The newsletter dealt with topics picked up during our field visits. We would deal with problems that we found teachers were actually struggling with in the field. I wrote the material in simple English. My Tanzanian co-worker then translated the material into simple Kiswahili.

It was a small newsletter – four pages of single-spaced materials, with illustrations. It was sent to all teachers on the project. Our hope was that it will be read with great interest. It was not! Even four pages of text was forbidding for these rural teachers. They had not read much of anything for some time. To read something that was not from the school book, to read without somebody guiding them, to read without somebody watching over them, was a most difficult task for them. They needed help from the outside to begin the process of becoming independent readers.

We instructed our supervisors to not merely distribute the newsletter to the teachers; we asked them to go through the newsletter with the teachers in a group as they came to collect their monthly honoraria. This introduction of the material to the teachers was necessary.

The *Sourcebook* will also need to be introduced to the teachers by their supervisors. Indeed, it is unlikely to be read by literacy teachers or their supervisors unless it is first read by the literacy specialists and literacy organizers in the project office in the district and in the headquarters above.

We suggest that organizers and specialists in a literacy programme should read the *Sourcebook* first, and then introduce it to supervisors in a series of short one- to two-day training seminars. In the same way, supervisors should introduce it to literacy teachers and instructors in another series of one- to two-day training sessions, spread over six months to a year. In the meantime, supervisors and teachers should both be encouraged to read the *Sourcebook* as much as they can.

Repeated readings and discussions of materials in the Sourcebook as well as the personal involvement of many people is important to construct the understandings that the *Sourcebook* can provide for undertaking effective programme actions.

THE NEED FOR ADAPTATIONS TO CULTURE AND CONTEXT

The theory and research included in this book comes from around the world. Western conceptions, definitions, theories and research are, however, predominant. It is important that material is put through filters of culture and context. Some of what is said may not be applicable in every culture as we go from Europe to Africa, and from Christian to Hindu or to Muslim communities. The context of literacy work is also important. What is usable in urban areas may not work in rural areas. What is meaningful for literacy in settled communities may not make sense in refugee camps.

LEARNING IN PEER GROUPS

In trying to speak to literacy teachers and workers all over the world, we had to be general. Clearly, if you are general, then you are not specific enough! Teachers will need to read the general material and learn to apply it to their specific situations. In this task they should not hesitate to take the help from others. For best results, this *Sourcebook* should be read and discussed in peer groups of teachers and supervisors. Together, in co-operation with each other, they will be able to help each other, and everybody will learn more than he or she would have learned alone. More important, they will be able to read it more critically and with greater sensitivity to culture and context.

The above implies that literacy workers in neighbouring communities should form professional networks. Networks of teachers will help them understand their own work better. Networks also create solidarity among literacy workers who work hard and long, often for so little.

ACKNOWLEDGEMENTS

Such books are never written by an author sitting alone in grand isolation. Many people make their own special contributions. It will require much space to list each and everyone who contributed to the writing of this book. I must, however, say thanks to Dr. Victor M. Ordoñez, Habib Mobarak and Jong-Gyu Kim for inviting me to write this book; and to Habib Mobarak particularly for supplying an initial list of chapters and contents most of which I was able to incorporate in this work. I am also thankful to many of my colleagues and friends who agreed to read this material and give me feedback on both structure and content. Among them I am pleased to mention Dr Josef Muller of the German Foundation for International Development, Bonn, Germany; Dr Steve Walter of the Summer Institute of Linguistics, Dallas, United States; Caroline Beverstock, co-author of *Adult Literacy – Contexts and Challenges* (published by the International Reading Association/ERIC in 1990); and Peter Magolda of the Department of Higher Education, School of Education, Indiana University.

H.S. Bhola
Indiana University

Chapter One

Adult Literacy, Literacy Teachers and Literacy Work

Even as readers open this *Sourcebook*, there will be questions. What is literacy? What is 'adult' literacy? Who teaches adult literacy? To whom? Where? When? What is adult literacy work like? What will adult literacy bring to those who learn and to those who teach it? What will literacy bring to the communities?

These are the kinds of questions that, we hope, you will be able to answer after reading this chapter.

The material in Chapter 1 will be presented in four parts.

- A basic definition of literacy

- The role and tasks of a literacy teacher

- Team work in functional literacy

- The scope and significance of literacy work.

WORDS OF WISDOM AND VOICES FROM THE REAL WORLD

The written word is the key to all freedoms. Reading and writing are our second birth. By making them available, we give life twice over. (François Nourissier in *Letters of Life*, Nathan/ UNESCO, 1991)

No difference could be more fundamental than that between peoples who can read and write and those who cannot. The latter have customs but no laws, techniques but no science, religion but no theology. (F. Musgrove in *Education and Anthropology: Other Cultures and the Teacher*, 1982)

THOUSANDS OF YEARS TOO LATE!

Literacy is unique amongst of human capacities. Yet the illiterate among us may be thousands of years too late in learning to read and write!

It was some 5000 years ago that first attempts were made to write. This was rather primitive writing, involving no more than making marks on a surface. The first form of writing, evolved in Mesopotamia around 3100 BC, is called Cuneiform. Cuneiform involved making signs and symbols with a wedge-like instrument on clay tablets. It is thought that trade was the mother of the invention of writing. As trade developed among countries in the region, so grew the need to keep shipping records.

At about the same time, the Egyptians were working with what are called hieroglyphics. The Semitic people on the Sinai peninsula developed the first true alphabet between 1500 and 1000 BC. This was an alphabet of consonants and had no vowels.

The Greeks added vowels.

How the idea of alphabets spread around the world is not known. Most alphabets today, except for Chinese characters, are built on similar principles.

The use of the alphabet was one direction in the development of writing. The other direction was logographic, leading to the Chinese system of writing. The Chinese system, the oldest in the world, may have been devised in the 2700s BC. The Chinese characters are symbols for whole words. It is thus a word-writing system.

The development of numerals (1, 2, 3, 4, 5, 6, 7, 8, 9) paralleled the development of alphabets. The writing of large numbers became possible with the invention of place values by mathematicians of ancient India. The mathematicians of India also invented the concept of zero. Zero (0) was used by the Indians as a mechanism to hold places in writing large numbers. Thus by merely using 3 and 0, in the right places, they could write 30, 303, 3003, 3030, 330033 and so on.

LITERACY WORK IS PART OF A GREAT TRADITION

In becoming literate and numerate, we are using the common genius of humanity that has taken 5000 years to develop to its present stage. In teaching literacy and numeracy to others, we are helping all humankind.

A basic definition of literacy

Literacy has become a fashionable word. These days all reading, in all settings, is called literacy. Children are not learning to read as they used to. They are now learning literacy. Adults are learning literacy as well. Then there is talk of cultural literacy, scientific literacy, political literacy and computer literacy.

READING IN SCHOOLS AND LITERACY OF ADULTS

Until a few years ago, the teaching of reading to children, in schools, was called the teaching of reading. The teaching of reading to adults, in out-of-school centres, or in night schools was called literacy teaching. It was a good idea to use two different words – reading and literacy – in these two different settings.

It was a good idea because children and adults are different people; they are different in age. They are different in experience; they carry different responsibilities; they are given different levels of respect by others; and they have to be dealt with differently in classes by teachers.

There are other differences. Children and adults are at different stages of life. As a result, they have different learning abilities. Also, their learning habits are different. They are interested in different subjects and content. Methods of teaching children and adults have to be somewhat different.

I wish that the word 'literacy' was not used to cover all kinds of reading – children and adults, inside and outside the school. I think it is confusing. In this *Sourcebook*, the word literacy is reserved for the teaching of reading to adults in settings outside the school. Thus, by literacy, we mean adult literacy.

A BASIC DEFINITION AND AN EXPANDED UNDERSTANDING OF LITERACY

A basic definition of literacy is 'the ability to read and write in the mother tongue'.

In the next chapter, we will see that this definition raises more questions than it answers. For example, it restricts literacy to literacy in the mother tongue. But what if the mother tongue is not a written language? Or if adults are already bilingual and the mother tongue is not so widely spoken? Or what if, in a newly independent country, literacy is available only in a foreign language?

Again, the basic definition does not talk about the levels of ability in reading and writing. We could go on to find other problems with the definition.

These and other questions of definitions are discussed in much greater detail in the next chapter. At this point, we should be satisfied with a basic definition of literacy as given above and with what we have called an expanded understanding of literacy.

This expanded understanding can be based on some general statements about literacy, such as:

- Literacy is not merely a skill, that is, the skill of reading and writing. It is a powerful potential – a quality with many uses –

given to individual men and women, boys and girls who become literate.

- Literacy makes it possible for individuals to use their minds in new and different ways. Ability to find and use new information gives them a new sense of freedom.

- Literacy is a social process. It brings the literate person new respect and social status. This happens even though other changes in their lives take more time.

- Literacy can and does bring development to societies.

We will return to these issues again.

The role and tasks of a literacy teacher

The literacy teacher is the most important person in a literacy pro-gramme. The roles and tasks of literacy teachers can be discussed at two levels: social and technical.

At the *social* (or cultural) level, the literacy teacher is a new player in most disadvantaged communities. These communities may have had a school teacher but not an adult-literacy teacher.

Since the literacy teacher affects the lives of adult men and women, his or her role is highly significant. The tasks of the literacy teacher at this level are those of an agent of community development. If these tasks are accomplished well, there will be cultural change and renewal. That is a big thing to happen!

At the *technical* level, the role of the literacy teacher is half-old and half-new. Literacy teachers teach – that is old. But they teach adults and they teach in new ways – that is new.

In this chapter, we discuss the role and tasks of the literacy teacher at the social level. The technical role of the literacy teacher is discussed in detail in Chapter 9.

AN EXPANDED ROLE FOR THE TEACHER

The role of the literacy teacher requires more than teaching. The teacher's role has indeed expanded and the teacher's tasks have multiplied.

Some literacy organizers want to call their teachers by another name. They want to call the teacher an 'animator' or a 'facilitator'.

One reason for this change is that the word 'teacher' is negative. They say that 'teacher' is an old-fashioned word and reminds people, both teachers and learners, of old-fashioned ways of teaching in schools.

They tell stories of literacy teachers that are both funny and tragic. I heard one such story myself. I was told of a literacy teacher in India who came to class with a stick in hand. He used the stick to punish adults twice his age! He could not imagine being a teacher without a stick. Of course, he was dismissed.

Other reasons for the change in language from teacher to animator, for example, are positive. The modern-day literacy teacher is not merely a teacher. He or she is also a community worker. In this expanded role, the teacher must animate (or motivate) the learners to learn. The teacher must also animate (or motivate) community leaders to take community actions. Hence it is best to call the teacher 'animator'. Note that this is part of the social role of the teacher.

There is yet another positive reason for the change from teacher to facilitator. For example, today's teacher is not seen as someone who knows everything. Today's teacher is seen as one who gives learners responsibility for their own learning. He or she also gives learners responsibility for making community decisions. Then, the teacher only facilitates learning and decision-making. Once again this is part of the social role of the literacy teacher.

You will find that we will use the word 'teacher' most of the time in this *Sourcebook*. That is so because the word 'teacher' is much more widely known than 'animator' or 'facilitator'. However, that does not mean that we believe in the old-world role of the teacher. Not at all! We strongly believe that the new teacher should indeed be an animator and a facilitator.

Some others refer to teachers as 'instructors'. In this *Sourcebook*, we do not use the word instructors to describe teachers, animators or facilitators. We reserve 'instructors' for 'trainers of teachers'.

VISUALIZING TEACHER'S PERFORMANCE

The teacher as teacher, animator or facilitator can be visualized to be performing his or her tasks as shown in Figures 1.1 and 1.2.

In Figure 1.1 the role and tasks of the teacher are essentially *technical*. These are discussed in greater detail in Chapter 9.

In Figure 1.2 we see the expanded role of the literacy teacher. The teacher now becomes an important actor in the community. The teacher is now an animator, facilitator, and development agent. The teacher deals with other development agents in the community – that is, extension workers from all other development ministries and departments such as agriculture, health and labour.

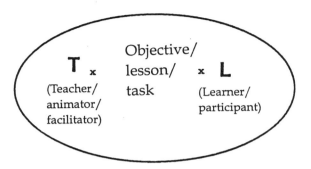

Figure 1.1 The basic teaching-learning relationship

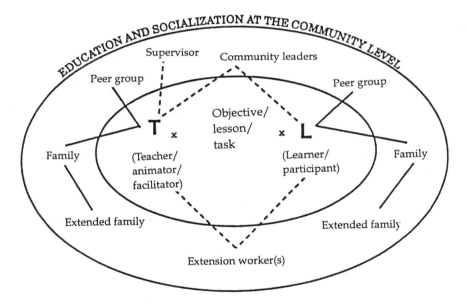

Figure 1.2 The basic teaching-learning relationship in the context of the community
Computer graphic by Kenichi Kubota, 1991

The teacher must himself or herself know fully the content of lessons to be taught, the instructional or development tasks to be accomplished and the nature of general objectives.

For successful work, the teacher must know his or her learners or participants as individuals. We dedicate at least one whole chapter to the topic of 'Understanding learners and their communities'.

Playing a social role to transform a community is a serious matter. The teacher must know himself or herself well to be able to play this new role ethically and effectively.

THE MEANING OF 'KNOW THYSELF!'

Self-knowledge is important both in life and work. Let us see what it can mean in the working life of a literacy teacher.

For self-knowledge, the teacher must understand his or her own personal needs, personal values, and personal abilities and potential.

FACING THE REALITY OF PERSONAL NEEDS

There is nothing wrong with having personal needs. However, personal needs must be faced honestly. They may be economic, psychological, social or political. When honestly faced, they may change in important ways. Self-interest and public interest need not always be at odds.

Economic needs. Literacy teachers are often volunteer teachers in rural areas. They do not get much from any source by way of money. Thus, for a school leaver turned teacher and living in the village, a few dollars in cash may be important. The teacher should ask: Am I in this work for a small sum of money? Or do I have greater expectations?

Psychological needs. Literacy teachers may have psychological needs of being around people and doing something useful in their lives. The teacher should ask: Am I in this work because I want to make friends? Or because I want to do something important in life?

Status needs. Literacy teachers may be aware of the social status that often comes from being a literacy teacher in a community. For example, in the United Republic of Tanzania literacy teachers received considerable respect from their learners. Teachers were addressed by their learners as *Mwalimu. Mwalimu* means 'teacher' in Kiswahili. President Nyerere himself was called *Mwalimu* by people who wanted to show him respect and affection. Literacy teachers were proud of being called *Mwalimu.*

It was observed that literacy teachers were also being invited to many weddings and beer parties because of their new social status in the community.

Political needs. There may also be political reasons for becoming literacy teachers. Someone may be working as a teacher because that will please the chief of the village. Another teacher may be working to obtain a leadership position for himself or herself in the community.

Understanding one's own personal needs is an important educational experience. One who understands his or her personal needs has better chances of achieving those needs. In the meantime, such a person can work on his or her teaching job with understanding. Both teachers' personal needs and the needs of learners are likely to be fulfilled.

CLARIFYING PERSONAL VALUES

Whatever we do involves our values. As literacy teachers our values underline all we do in and outside the classroom.

Gender-values. Gender-values are important. For example, if male teachers (or even female teachers) have values that consider women inferior, they may treat female learners badly. They might make them sit at the back of class or treat them with contempt. They will, therefore, not teach them well because they will expect less from them.

Racial values. Racial and ethnic biases appear in the classrooms among learners. Teachers can also possess negative values towards some ethnic and racial groups. Learners from such racial groups or a minority tribe can be mistreated and badly taught. Their education can be seriously neglected.

Occupational values. Teachers of adults acquire important occupational values. It is these occupational values that lead us to label literacy teachers, 'facilitators'; adult classes, 'groups'; and adults in literacy groups, 'learners' rather than 'students'.

Occupational values are a serious matter. Literacy teachers who are also teaching children during the day will have to make special efforts to overcome their occupational values to deal with adults effectively. These teachers should not be treating adult learners like children; they should treat them as equals. Teachers who are teaching after retirement from the army may want too much order, discipline and obedience, again because of occupational values learned in the army.

What to do about values? Values, of course, can not be changed like one changes clothes. However, knowing what one's values are helps. The process of individual change always starts with self-awareness.

Values worth promoting. There are some important human values which play important roles in human relations and in teaching. These are: all individuals – rich and poor, young and old, sick and healthy – have individual worth and dignity as living beings; everyone is entitled to loving acceptance, respect and trust; and, both in word and deed, to build others' sense of self-worth and self-esteem. These issues are considered again in Chapter 8.

UNDERSTANDING OWN ABILITIES AND PERSONAL POTENTIAL

Finally, it is important for literacy teachers to have realistic understandings of their own abilities and personal potential.

Not pretending to be an instant expert. When someone is given the job of a literacy teacher, all one gets is an 'official designation'. On the first day of acquiring that designation, the person with the new designation may know nothing at all about being a literacy teacher. To pretend to have become an expert teacher instantly is foolish indeed.

Typically, all literacy teachers receive some kind of training. Teacher-trainees should make the very best of their training. Some literacy teachers think that after their training there is nothing more to learn. Nothing could be farther from the truth.

Being a continuing learner of subject matter and methods. The teacher must continue to learn about both new subject matter and new methods. The teacher must continue to reflect upon his or her daily experiences in the classroom and the community. Teachers who teach adults to read must set an example. They must read widely and well. They must become lifelong learners. This *Sourcebook* should help you in the tasks of being a good teacher.

Inter-learning among teachers and learners. It is important for the teacher to have a realistic view of his or her own abilities. The fact of being appointed a teacher does not make one more able, more experienced and wiser than everybody in the class and the community. There may be wiser heads in the class. There may be more able people – among our learners – ready to be discovered.

The teacher's task is to guide those who need guidance. But a good teacher uses the abilities and experience of those in class who seem to have more of both. Teachers should name some of their students as associate teachers. Let there be mutual teaching and peer learning. Teachers, together with their adult learners, must participate in defining problems, gathering information, making choices and applying solutions in resolving those problems.

No limits to learning. Teachers must be realistic about their abilities, but they should be generous in estimating their future potential. They should know that there is no limit to learning. The teacher of functional literacy has the possibility of knowing a lot about agricultural knowledge, about poultry farming, about health and nutrition, about house building and about a hundred other subjects. The literacy teacher has the potential to become an effective teacher and a persuasive leader. There are no limits to his or her learning. The potential is limitless.

Team work in functional literacy

The literacy teacher is always a member of a larger team. Some on the team, the teacher will have met in person; some will have helped the teacher from a distance.

THE TEAM IN THE FIELD

The literacy teacher working in a 'functional' literacy programme can not work alone. This is so because in functional literacy, literacy is combined with the learning of economic skills.

At the very least, the functional literacy teacher must work with extension workers who are promoting development in the community and are working with learners on various income generating activities. Typically, these extension workers will include the agricultural extension worker, the health educator, the nutritionist and the family planning worker. The teacher will perhaps invite these extension workers to his classes and will organize demonstrations.

An even more important role can be assumed for the functional literacy teacher. That role will mean making the literacy class the nerve centre for all extension work in the community.

THE DISTANT TEAM

By the distant team, we mean those people who make it possible for the literacy teacher to teach effectively. These include: literacy organizers at the national, state and district levels; programme development and curriculum development specialists; instructional materials and media specialists; the training specialist; evaluation specialists; post-literacy work organizers; and, of course, literacy supervisors (Figure 1.3).

Figure 1.4 puts the whole thing within a social context. At this stage, the literacy teacher should not be worried about fully understanding the total literacy system. The teacher need not try to remember the names and labels for these many subsystems, nor try to learn about the roles and tasks of the actors within these subsystems. A general appreciation of the scope and the complexity of the literacy system is enough.

For the moment, therefore, please read through the material quickly, remembering that there is more to literacy work than teaching of reading and writing to a group of adults.

THE LITERACY SYSTEM IS AN IDEAL-TYPE SYSTEM

The system represented here is an ideal-type system. Not all literacy projects, programmes or campaigns are lucky enough to have all these components.

All these subsystems work through the actors within those subsystems. All the subsystems interact with each other. In other words, they influence each other in a variety of ways, sometimes directly, sometimes exerting indirect and weak influences.

If there is not much interaction among subsystems of a literacy system, that means the system is unhealthy. Such a system will need renewal – bringing everyone together to work together selflessly.

The ideological subsystem clarifies the cultural and economic ideas on which the literacy project is based. It then shows how these ideas (that is, the ideology) of the literacy programme relates to the politics of the country.

The policy and planning subsystem connects ideology with concrete policies and plans of the literacy system. For example, what regions and what groups should benefit first?

The institution-building and organizational subsystem makes decisions about sharing responsibility between government and non-government agencies. It decides about structures of participation by the people by organizing literacy projects, regional ornational programmes, or small or large campaigns. It decides what new institutions should be created and how old institutions should be networked.

The mobilizational subsystem makes decisions about mobilization of teachers to teach and of learners who should come to learn. It also seeks to mobilize resources of communities on the one hand and of the state on the other hand.

The professional support subsystem provides professional support to the literacy system for training, evaluation and research. Part of such a subsystem may be within the primary literacy organization. Part may come from the universities and research institutions.

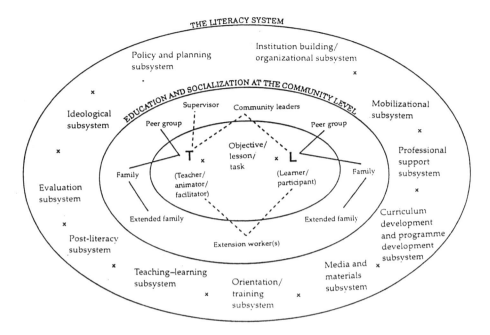

Figure 1.3 Teaching and learning in the context of an ideal-type, fully functioning literacy system

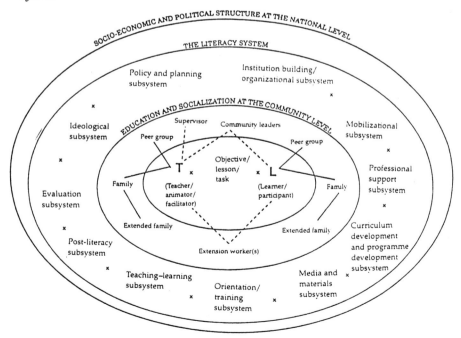

Figure 1.4 The basic Teaching-learning relationship within the total social-technical system

The curriculum development and programme development subsystem makes curricular judgements about what will be taught, at what levels and in what sequence. It also ensures programme delivery.

The media and materials subsystem makes decisions about writing and publishing primers, follow-up books, visual aids, teachers guides and manuals. Such a subsystem must also work for integrating various materials and media available from a variety of inside and outside sources.

The orientation and training subsystem prepares pre-service and in-service training programmes for teachers and supervisors, and orientation programmes for other personnel.

The teacher-learner subsystem makes sure that the heart of any literacy system, the teaching-learning subsystem, is successful.

The post-literacy subsystem undertakes all actions that will ensure that newly literate adults keep on reading so that they do not relapse into illiteracy. More important, the organizers of the post-literacy subsystem must ensure that the newly literate make use of literacy in the economic, social, political and cultural aspects of daily life.

The evaluation subsystem seeks to ensure that all decisions made within the literacy subsystem are 'informed' decisions. That means collection of both descriptive and evaluative information. Evaluative information must be both quantitative and qualitative. Learning achievement as the impact of programmes on communities should also be studied. All evaluation should be collaborative and participative.

Literacy supervisors are the link between literacy teacher and others in the professional programme system. They visit teachers in their centres to guide and encourage them.

The scope and significance of literacy work

Knowing the big picture always helps. We already know about the team of which the literacy teacher is a part. We know that the functional literacy team includes other educators, extension workers, media people and community leaders. In this section, we discuss the size and scope of literacy work within an even larger context of the society.

Before talking about the size and scope of literacy work, let us talk about the sponsorship of literacy work.

In the Third World, literacy work is often sponsored by the state. There are some literacy analysts who do not like literacy work by the state; they suspect that state-directed literacy programmes serve those in power and that state-run programmes do not serve the interests of the people. This may be true some of the time. However, the state need not always be considered to be anti-people.

In some countries, the state may have become oppressive and insensitive to the interests of the people. In such cases, the opposition or the underground can arise and may undertake literacy work. Again, in such countries, through literacy work, opposition movements and the underground may organize people in behalf of people's interest against the excesses of the state. Literacy work may be one of their tactics.

Finally, there are organizations described as non-governmental organizations or private voluntary organizations which may undertake literacy work. These organizations may draw some or all of their money from the state, yet they may serve the people's interests better.

Non-governmental organizations have now developed a particular ideology about literacy work. They seek to serve popular interests. They use collaborative planning and participative methodologies of implementation and evaluation. They claim flexibility in outreach and of approach, and argue that they serve people neglected by the state.

Non-governmental organizations are seldom able to run nationwide programmes or campaigns; their dependence on state resources restricts their freedom.

THE SIZE AND SCOPE OF LITERACY WORK AND MODES OF DELIVERY

Surely your literacy class is not the only class in the country! If your village is big enough, there may other literacy classes in your own village. If you are working in a large factory, or in a mine, there may be many more literacy classes going on at the same time. Depending on their size and scope, literacy effort may be called projects, programmes or campaigns. Three approaches to literacy work are defined here.

Literacy projects. Literacy classes may be parts of small projects. Projects typically cover a cluster of villages, one large factory or one mining site. Their clients are easily identifiable and their objectives are clear-cut. Projects typically have a single sponsor. They are self-contained and seldom in touch with other projects.

Literacy programmes. Literacy programmes are larger in scale than literacy projects. They may cover a whole country, or a large region within the country. They may focus on some client groups, but they do not exclude anyone. Programme objectives are more general, although local people may add local objectives. Programmes are typically sponsored by the state. They always invite participation from individuals, communities and organizations. However, co-ordination of efforts is seldom success-ful.

Literacy campaigns. Literacy campaigns are often larger than literacy programmes. They may cover a whole country. Literacy campaigns may serve as umbrellas to cover several programmes and projects under the one campaign. Campaigns are typically people's programmes. They seek to serve everyone, including women and speakers of non-standard languages. Campaign objectives are therefore also typically general. Again, local people can add local objectives. One distinction between a campaign and a programme is the style of mobilization. Campaigns have *red hot* commitments from politicians. Campaigns always involve large-scale mobilization efforts. The masses are encouraged to join in – to learn, to teach, to organize.

As a literacy teacher in your community, you should know that you are part of a larger effort. There are others, perhaps, spread all over the country, who are engaged in the similar effort. You are thus part of a larger group, a larger mission. That should give you a sense of solidarity with other literacy workers.

THE SIGNIFICANCE OF LITERACY WORK

It is also important to know that the literacy class that you struggle with day after day has larger significance. This is not the place to give you a 'theory' that proves the role of literacy in development. However, literacy teachers must understand literacy and must be able to argue for literacy.

Professor V. Eswara Reddy of Osmania University in Hyderabad, India, did a lot of literacy work in Andhra Pradesh, India. He found that many literacy teachers and workers themselves were apparently uncon-vinced about literacy – they could not say anything convincing about literacy to village leaders or to potential learners who were unsure of the usefulness of literacy.

Would-be participants in literacy groups often do not know what use literacy would be to them. They talk of being old. They talk of being unable to find a job after they have become literate. Some who join the classes leave later. They see nothing concrete at the end of classes. The tragic thing is that literacy teachers have nothing much to say by way of answers. They themselves were unconvinced.

We will now give some simple statements that help convince doubters of the significance of adult literacy. These statements can be used in answering questions and in laying fears of would-be learners to rest.

1. Convince adult learners that they are not too old to learn. Tell them that adults can learn as easily as children. Indeed, adults already know 'how to learn' and do much better than children in learning to read.

2. Help adult learners to understand that it is never too late to begin to learn. Tell them that they have long and productive lives ahead of them and that they must become literate for the sake of their families; they must set an example for their children.

3. Some adult learners may tell you that they do not want literacy because a little of it will not get them a job. Tell them that it is not necessary or wise to connect literacy with a job. We try to eat well even if eating well will not get us a job. We try to keep good health, even though we can not always convert our good health into a job. We like to go to church or pray in a mosque or a temple even if it would not end in a job. Why do we have to connect literacy with a job right away? In today's world everyone needs literacy. It helps us live better at home, work better in the vegetable garden and keep our children healthy. What could be a better 'job' than that?

4. Literacy cannot wait because children cannot carry the burden of the illiteracy of their parents. They cannot come home to do their parents' reading, writing and counting. As for the children themselves, it will be years before they enter economic, social and political life.

5. Do not think that we are living in oral environments. The so-called oral environments are long gone. We already live in literate environments. Adults who are literate can read messages in their environment, for example, signs on roads, shops, buses, toilets, etc. Even in rural areas, the uses of literacy are many and they are expanding day by day.

6. Adults who are literate can read safety signs at work in the factory and on the farm.

7. Adults who are literate can read development literature on productivity, on food production, on health and nutrition, and on family planning.

8. Adults who are literate can read the newspaper for information and books for entertainment.

9. Adults who are literate can read the scriptures to fulfil their spiritual needs.

10. Adults who can read do not feel dependent, but feel free. They talk of 'losing blindness', and 'coming out of darkness into light'.

11. Adults who can read and use their literacy skills become better informed and, therefore, feel more confident. Those around them respect them and attribute to them higher status.

12. Adults who can read can assume community leadership because they can take notes, and write agendas and minutes of meetings.

13. Adults who can read make better decisions at work, on the farm, at election time and at home in the enjoyment of leisure.

14. When adults make better decisions at home, life at home changes. Literate men are more likely to treat their wives as equals. Literate wives transform the health and well-being of the family.

15. When adults make better decisions at work, there are fewer accidents, better co-operation, greater productivity and movement towards economic democracy. Economic democracy means that workers participate in decision-making and share in gains from higher productivity.

16. When adults make better decisions at election time, the politics of the community changes for the better.

17. Things add up. When all – or most – adults, both men and women, make better decisions at home, at work, at election time and at leisure, things add up to freedom, fairness and personal fulfilment. Infant mortality drops. If the mother is literate, children are sure to be enrolled in school. That is real development!

REWARDS FOR TEACHERS OF ADULT LITERACY

Literacy teachers may not receive great financial rewards. But there is no limit to non-monetary rewards. They shape individual lives. They shape communities. They shape countries. They shape history.

THINGS TO DO OR THINK ABOUT

1. How will you describe the literacy initiative on which you are working currently? What is its sponsorship – state, non-governmental organization or some combination? What is its size and scope – a project, a programme or a campaign?

2. What is the definition of literacy as found in the records and documents of your literacy project, programme or campaign? Does the definition match with actual practice?

3. Has an adult learner ever told you that literacy is useless? What did you reply?

4. In this chapter, we have included arguments that we think you can use in persuading adults to join literacy classes and to begin using literacy in their daily lives. Do you think that you can improve upon this argument? What will you add?

5. As a literacy teacher, have you ever given thought to your personal purposes for joining the literacy initiative as a teacher?

6. Do you feel rewarded in any way through the opportunity of becoming an adult literacy teacher?

7. I hope you have looked at Figure 1.4 with due care. Do you realize that primary school education also has a similar ideal-type system? Do you realize that the agricultural extension worker and the health educator are also part of similar systems?

Many Faces of Literacy

Literacy is difficult to define. Its meanings tend to slip away. The concept of literacy is indeed elusive.

Questions arise. Literacy in what language? At what level? Literacy for what expected use? To read stories, to read scriptures, to read a leaflet to grow more food, or to read instructions to run a machine? To write letters, to keep accounts, to read and sign a contract, or to serve a legal notice? To run a business? To vote?

These are the questions we seek to answer in this chapter. We talk of the many faces of literacy; we discuss the many different definitions of literacy. Special attention is given to defining the concept and programme of functional literacy.

We show that a universal definition of literacy is almost impossible. We will suggest that each literacy project, programme or campaign will have to have its own definition of literacy. Such a definition will have to be relevant to special objectives and particular contexts.

This chapter is broken down into four discussion elements.

- Literacy – skills and subject matter
- Many definitions of literacy
- The necessity for our very own definition of literacy
- Functional literacy – the concept and the programme.

WORDS OF WISDOM AND VOICES FROM THE REAL WORLD

Literacy is a part of the 'Awakening' of the people...and is necessary to build a critical mass of spiritual consciousness. (Dr. A.T. Ariyarante, *President of Sarvodaya Shramadana Movement, Sri Lanka*)

The illiterate people of the world are caught in a vicious circle; the illiterate are poor, the poor are powerless, and the powerless are illiterate, and so on.

A 12-year-old girl who had lost her father and whose mother worked washing and selling plastic was taken away for prostitution by people who told her mother that she will help the family finances. When I told her mother to go to the police, she refused in order to avoid any attacks by the agents. Lawyers are of course out of the question for people like her. This is a case which is not at all unusual in the slums.

This is the reality of the illiterate. Literacy is not just teaching how to read and write; it is providing opportunities for people to protect themselves. (Mrs. Prateep Ungsongtham Hata, *Executive Secretary of Duan Prateep Foundation, Thailand*)

Literacy – skills and subject matter

We do not just 'read'. We always read 'something'. That means that in literacy, *skills* of reading and the *subject matter* of what is read are always combined. Skills and subject matter are inseparable.

THE SKILLS OF READING

To read, we need reading *skills*. We need to recognize letters that make syllables and syllables that make words.

All alphabetical systems are not of the same difficulty level. Arabic letters may be more difficult to learn than Roman letters. Combining Arabic letters into words is more complex. The Chinese ideograms are the most difficult to master even by the native speakers of Chinese.

There is, of course, more to reading skills than recognizing letters, syllables, words and characters. We need to know the language and the written form of language. While reading sentences, we need to be able to pause at the right places, with or without the help of punctuation marks.

We need to be able to move down the lines on the page without losing our place. We should be able to go from one line to the next. We should not keep on returning to the same line or skip a line or two. We need to learn to anticipate the form of sentences even as we begin reading them. An experienced reader is able to do all that.

THE SUBJECT MATTER OF READING

Remember, we do not just read; we always read something. That means that subject matter is inseparable from our level of skills in reading.

But subject matter can vary. The subject matter of a romance novel is different from the subject matter of an economics textbook. A textbook on economics is generally harder to read than a novel. A book of astronomy may be even more difficult to read than a book on economics.

The same subject matter can present different levels of difficulty in reading. A college textbook on economics will be harder than a high school textbook on economics. The less the reader knows of the subject, the harder it will be to read.

There is another important matter hidden in subject matter. Subject matter can be technical and professional. It can talk of how to grow tomatoes, about childcare and about safety in mines.

Alternatively, the subject matter can be obviously ideological. It can talk of ignorance, of hunger, of injustice. Indeed, the technical and the ideological are impossible to separate completely.

It should be clear from the above that to develop a standard definition of literacy will be difficult. It is in fact an impossible task. Languages differ. Levels of reading skills differ. Subject matter differs. Contexts of use differ. How could we have a standard and universal definition of literacy?

Many definitions of literacy

There are many definitions of literacy around. It is easy to understand why?.

- Literacy definitions are different, because the languages of literacy are different: Chinese *versus* Hindi.

- Literacy definitions are different because different levels and standards of literacy skills are possible: some can read better and faster than others even when they are in the same grade.

- Literacy definitions are different because people prepare themselves to read different kinds of subject matter: historians *versus* logicians.

- Literacy definitions are different because people differ in their objectives: workplace literacy *versus* literacy for liberation.

A cultural definition of literacy. In the 1960s, UNESCO defined literacy as 'the ability to read and write in the mother tongue'. Notice the emphasis on the mother tongue.

This definition was proposed when many of the countries in Africa and Asia were still colonized. Colonial rulers in Africa and elsewhere taught literacy to their native subjects in English, French, German, Portuguese and Afrikaans. The natives were, of course, learning nothing much.

Thus, UNESCO thought it was necessary to propose this definition. It can be called a cultural definition of literacy as well as a political definition of literacy. This definition talked of skills, but it said nothing about the level of skills of reading and writing.

Another UNESCO definition of literacy. Another definition of literacy had appeared in a UNESCO document in 1958. It stated that 'a person is *illiterate* who cannot with understanding both read and write a short, simple statement on everyday life'.

There are obvious problems with this definition. How short a sentence will be acceptable? What is a simple statement? People's everyday lives differ. The everyday life of an urban worker makes other demands than the everyday life of a village farmer. Whose everyday life is typical? Finally, who judges whether or not a simple statement has been read and understood satisfactorily?

UNESCO's current definition of literacy. A more recent set of definitions included in UNESCO documents should be of interest:

'A person is *literate* who can with understanding both read and write a short simple statement on his everyday life.

'A person is *illiterate* who cannot with understanding both read and write a short simple statement on his everyday life.

'A person is *functionally literate* who can engage in all those activities in which literacy is required for effective functioning of his group and community and also for enabling him to continue to use reading, writing and calculation for his own and the community's development.

'A person is *functionally illiterate* who can engage in all those activities in which literacy is required for effective functioning of his group and community and also for enabling him to continue to use reading, writing and calculation for his own and the community's development.'

Problems remain with the above definitions as well, because they tie literacy to its use in particular communities around the world. The question of levels was again avoided.

It should be noted also that the meanings of the term 'functional' as used here have changed over the years. In the definition above, functionality is 'general'. It covers all the functions necessary for community life. In the new definition of functionality, there is a clear and marked focus on *economic* functions. In this *Sourcebook* as well functionality will have a strong economic bias.

An essential definition of literacy. Sarah Gudchinsky, a well-known linguist who worked with the Summer Institute of Linguistics for many many years, catches the essence of literacy in her definition:

A person is literate who 'can read and understand everything he would have understood if it had been spoken to him; and can write, so that it can be read, anything he can say'.

This definition includes both reading and writing, but no special reference is made to numeracy. It should also be noted that Sarah Gudchinsky is talking of the pre-literate's natural language of speech, that is, the mother tongue.

Keith Levine puts Gudchinsky's definition in new words when he defines literacy as 'the capacity to acquire and exchange information via the written word'. The definition can be stretched to include numeracy.

Literacy of marks. More recently, the author of this book, has talked of 'the literacy of marks'. This literacy of marks includes 'the literacy of alphabets'. The new literacy of marks, has been defined as:

'the ability of a person ... to code and decode, that is, read and write, a living and growing system of marks – words, numbers, notations, schematas and diagramatic representations – all of which have become part of the visual language of the people...both the specialist and the non-specialist.'

Indeed, traffic signs, signs at airports, danger signals, notations, schematas and maps are marks that have become unofficial members of all the world's alphabet systems. It is not possible to read the map depicted in Figure 2.1 without the literacy of marks that we have talked about.

This definition of literacy expands the scope of literacy of alphabets. It draws attention to other sign systems and written symbols in the environment. But it does not solve the problem of level and standardization of skills.

Traditional literacy. A UNESCO document gives this definition: '*Traditional literacy* training has only one *intrinsic* objective, namely, the teaching of reading and writing, accompanied in most cases by elementary arithmetic. It is thus an isolated, extracurricular operation which is self-justifying and an end in itself.'

Key

A1 PIKE BUILDING
Classrooms, Library, Telephone
Workroom, Switchboard, International
Academic Bookstore

A2 MAHLER BUILDING
TXSIL School Office, ICW, TAC, IRAC, ILC,
Inc., Center Director

A3 HUNT BUILDING
Academic Personnel, Academic
Publications, Admissions, Anthropology,
Center Media, Dallas Computer Services,
Int'l Computer Coodinator, Literacy,
Printing Arts, Security, Sociolinguistics,
Translation, VP Academic Affairs

A4 International Administration Building

B1 Museum

B2 Activities Center, Child Care

B3 Finance and Staff

B4 Staff

B5 Dorm

C1a-f STAFF OFFICES
Center Services, Housing, Center
Personnel, Assistant Chaplain, Member
Services Advisor, Coord. for Personnel
Planning, VP Personnel, Chaplain,
Management Training, LAAD,
International Archiving,
Executive Vice President,
Public Affairs, Project Funding,
Int'l Information Services,
Townsend Institute Staff,
International candidate
Secretary, Printshop, Int'l
Personnel, Int'l PFA

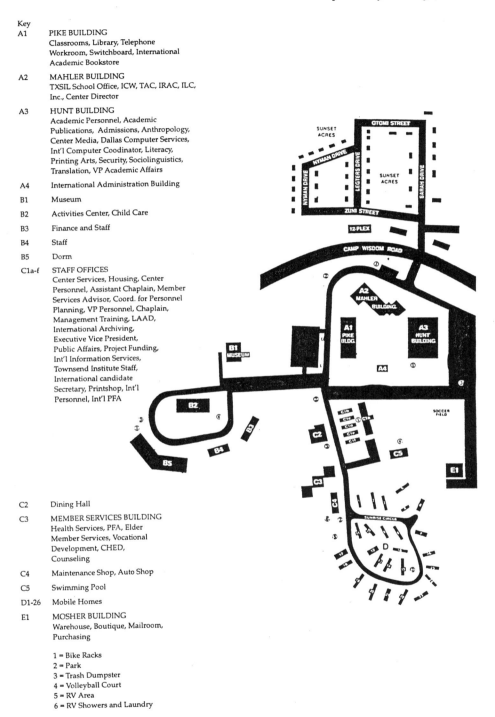

C2 Dining Hall

C3 MEMBER SERVICES BUILDING
Health Services, PFA, Elder
Member Services, Vocational
Development, CHED,
Counseling

C4 Maintenance Shop, Auto Shop

C5 Swimming Pool

D1-26 Mobile Homes

E1 MOSHER BUILDING
Warehouse, Boutique, Mailroom,
Purchasing

1 = Bike Racks
2 = Park
3 = Trash Dumpster
4 = Volleyball Court
5 = RV Area
6 = RV Showers and Laundry

Figure 2.1

One can hear negative overtones of the above definition. It is seen as isolated, even backward. Traditional literacy is somehow seen as without purpose: literacy for literacy's sake!

Traditional literacy is also assumed to use traditional methods of teaching literacy skills. It is seen to be insensitive to the importance of the subject matter of literacy lessons. In subject matter, typically, traditional themes are used. Primers may use sentences such as the following:

God is great.

Father is smoking.

Mother is cooking.

Children are playing.

Cultural literacy. Cultural literacy also has undergone changes of meanings. In its earlier meanings, cultural literacy was the approach used by Christian missionaries from the West in their literacy work in the colonies. It selected some existing cultural patterns while rejecting others. It introduced new cultural values to promote religious conversions.

In its new meanings, cultural literacy is radical. It means pride in the learners' culture. It means active enjoyment of the culture. It means the continuous rebirth of indigenous cultures in the lives of people.

Civic literacy. Civic literacy is literacy for good citizenship. Citizenship involves both duties and rights. Some civic literacy programmes emphasize duties and forget about peoples' rights. Some may be doing the opposite: emphasizing rights and not duties. A balance is, of course, necessary. At a deeper level, civic literacy means a shared understanding of the approach to life of a group of people.

Functional literacy. You might remember a statement we made earlier, that all literacy is functional. How can literacy not acquire a function? Yet we do have an approach to literacy called 'functional literacy'.

The concept of 'functional literacy' has changed its meaning over the years. At first, functionality had a general meaning – the ability to function effectively in a particular cultural context.

At a UNESCO conference in Tehran in 1965, functional literacy was tied directly and tightly to economic functions. Functional literacy was based on the psychology of an adult at work. The teaching of reading and of economic skills were to be integrated. The integration was to be so good that the learners would experience the two teachings as one learning.

In the late 1960s and early 1970s, economic functionality seemed to have gone crazy. It was in reaction to this that different voices were raised against economic functionality. These new voices talked of *empowering* people, not merely making them more useful to their employers and more functional within the economy.

Critical literacy. Critical literacy (also called emancipatory or transformational literacy) is radical literacy. The purpose of this literacy is to empower people, to help them reclaim culture, community, beliefs and knowledge. It aims to make people masters of their destiny.

Critical literacy enables people to become critical of what they see, of what they hear, of what they get and of what they are asked to give. In other words, they become critically aware of the social, political and economic relationships in which they are caught. Critical literacy comes closest to political education. Critical literacy wants people to do something with their newly acquired literacy skills. It seeks to organize people for political action for transforming the world around them.

Paulo Freire catches the relationship between reading and doing, that is, between literacy work and empowering work, thus:

> 'Reading the world always precedes reading the word, and reading the word implies continuously reading the world... In a way, however, we can go further and say that reading the word is not preceded merely by reading the world, but by a certain form of writing it or rewriting it, that is, of transforming it by means of conscious, practical work. For me, this dynamic movement is central to the literacy process.'

The interest in critical literacy and literacy for empowering has not fully won over the functional literacy approach. Indeed, functional literacy with emphasis on economic functionality is appearing and reappearing in many forms.

Workplace literacy. Workplace literacy is to the industrialized West what functional literacy is to the Third World. Literacy skills and subject matter are both linked to the workplace of learners. The literacy requirements of the job or jobs being done by workers are analysed. A curriculum is then developed that can teach those skills. The approach is highly utilitarian. There is, however, the expectation that skills learned in workplace literacy will be transferred to other settings.

The use of computers in teaching workplace literacy is quite popular in the United States of America for at least two reasons: American businesses are familiar with the use of technology and putting workplace literacy programmes on computers is cheaper for business and industry than employing teachers or trainers.

Task-specific literacy. Task-specific literacy is functionality carried to its extreme. It ties learning of reading and writing to specific tasks to be performed by an adult. Adults who need to read a pattern for tailoring to make a dress are taught to read that pattern. Adults who need to get a driving licence are taught to read to pass the driving test.

Inter-generational literacy/family literacy. Literacy, it is now well understood, is a social process. Illiterate parents cannot teach the value of being literate to their children. Thus, their children are likely to grow up illiterate.

The above has led to a focus on inter-generational literacy. The idea is to teach literacy to both generations – to parents and children. The two can then inspire, encourage and strengthen each other.

The idea of inter-generational literacy has grown naturally into the idea of family literacy. Literacy workers are now trying to teach literacy to families rather than an individual parent or to a youth who cannot read and write.

There may be yet other definitions of literacy. The point to remember is that different definitions use different mixes of skills and subject matter depending upon their needs and values. No definition is acceptable as a universal and standard definition.

The necessity for our very own definition of literacy

The above discussion establishes the impossibility of one universal standardized definition of literacy. But there is another important implication in the above discussion – the necessity of having our very own definition of literacy. Each literacy project, programme or campaign needs to do that. It needs to come up with its own particular definition of literacy in its particular setting.

AMERICAN DEFINITION OF FUNCTIONAL LITERACY

In the United States official definitions of literacy have been based on levels of reading skills presumed to be acquired at various levels in the formal school.

When the government was recruiting young people for the army at the beginning of the Second World War, a Grade 4 level of literacy was considered functional. (We are using the word functional in its old meaning and not in the new meaning of economic functionality.) In the

1980s, functional literacy in the United States had come to mean literacy skills at Grade 12 level. The 1986 National Assessment of Educational Progress (NAEP) in the United States used a framework that accepted the following definition of literacy: 'Literacy is the ability to use printed and written information to function in society, to achieve one's goals, and to develop one's knowledge and potential'.

This general definition was made concrete by developing two complete sets of tests, each consisting of the following three tests:

The prose literacy test measures the skills and knowledge needed to read and interpret materials such as newspaper articles, magazines and books.

The document literacy test measures the skills and knowledge needed to identify and use information located in materials such as charts, forms, tables and indexes.

The quantitative literacy test measures the skills and knowledge needed to apply arithmetic operations to information contained in printed materials such as a loan or sale advertisement, an order form or a chequebook.

A PROGRAMME-SPECIFIC DEFINITION: THE CASE OF INDIA

We have indicated above the necessity of establishing our very own definitions of literacy in our various projects, programmes and campaigns. The Indian National Programme of Adult Education defined 'literacy by objective' as follows:

SPECIFICATION OF NORMS FOR LITERACY ATTAINMENT

(1) *Reading skills*

    i. The learner should, at the end of the programme, be able to read orally – so pronouncing correctly a simple passage of about five to six sentences in a minute. Such a passage may be from the reading material, used at the centre and should be preferably in the same letter type.

    ii. The learner should be able to read approximately ten to twenty words, of hand-written (bold) material, per minute.

    iii. The learner should be able to read with understanding road signs, posters, simple instructions and some headlines of newspapers for neo-literates.

    iv. The learner should be able to read figures from 1 to 100.

v. The learner should be able to comprehend the material read in items i, ii and iii above, and should be able to answer questions relating to it.

(2) *Writing skills*

i. The learner should be able to copy out a minimum of ten words per minute from a small passage. The words in the passage may be of not more than four letters. They should also be able to understand what is written.

ii. The learner should be able to take down dictation at the speed of at least seven words per minute.

iii. The learner should be able to write on a straight line with proper spacing on ruled paper.

(3) *Computational skills*

i. The learner should be able to make minor calculation of up to three digit figures involving simple addition, subtraction, multiplication, division; the divisor in case of division and multiplier in case of multiplication should be one digit.

ii. At the end of the course the learner should be in a position to gain a practical knowledge of metric weights and measures.

iii. The learner should be able to know tables up to ten.

(4) *Application of literacy skills*

i. The learner should be able to read captions, signboards (written road-signs), posters, newspaper headlines and other communications that come to him in legible and bold handwritten papers.

ii. The learner should be able to write simple letters and simple applications, and fill up forms such as money orders and loan and bank forms.

iii. The learner should be able to keep accounts of the day-to-day expenditure and savings, and be able to check entries in their post office or bank pass-book.

iv. The learner should be able to follow and act upon instructions given on bags of fertilizers, pesticides, seeds, medicines, etc.

Such operational definitions of adult literacy can be used for a variety of purposes: for curriculum development, for the design of management information systems and for learner evaluation. While teaching-learning within an adult group, definitions such as the above should be adapted to the groups needs.

As we have mentioned before, the widely accepted, UNESCO-supported 1965 definition of functional literacy is rooted in economic functions. But dissatisfaction with the definition started even at its birth. Focus on 'bread alone' was disliked. At the same time Paulo Freire's work became very influential, and Freire talked of literacy for liberation, not merely training of labour.

A middle way to functional literacy has now emerged. We will talk about it in the next section.

Functional literacy – the concept and the programme

The current concept of functional literacy, as we indicated above, is more than mere economic skills. It has come to have three elements: literacy, functionality and awareness.

The *literacy component* focuses on the skills of reading and writing. The acceptable level of skills for literacy have to be decided within each project, programme or campaign. Of course, we can never separate skills from subject matter.

The *functionality component* deals with economic skills. Good functional literacy programmes do not merely teach and demonstrate economic skills. Economic skills are typically taught within the context of 'income generating' projects. Thus, participants are able to earn some money.

The *awareness component* creates awareness among learners in regard to their social, cultural and political life. Thus, it is a mixture of cultural and civic literacy.

Experience tells us that awareness is not easy to teach. Too often it degenerates into 'public relations' work for government programmes. At its best, however, it can teach people to shape their social and political life, and to take pride in their cultures (Figure 2.2).

The functional literacy triangle (literacy, functionality and awareness) is, of course, interested in subject matter. It wants to make people knowledge-rich. It seeks to build the knowledge capital of families, communities and countries. It is no wonder that the concept of functionality has

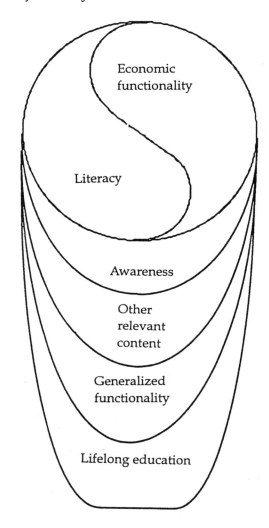

Figure 2.2 Visualizing functional literacy curriculum
Computer graphic by Kenichi Kubota, 1991

been generalized to include basic education. Generally basic education is defined as the basic level and content of education that everyone in a society must have. Functional literacy programmes seek to provide that basic level of skills and content.

There can be no universal and standard syllabuses for basic education. Good basic education programmes seek to cover the following:

- Cultural education
- History

- Political systems
- Occupational skills
- Scientific knowledge
- Human relations
- Race Relations.

FUNCTIONAL LITERACY AND LIFELONG EDUCATION

When carried to its logical conclusion, generalized functionality becomes lifelong education. An effective functional literacy programme should be linked with lifelong education for all.

Lifelong education means that education has no end, education does not finish with finishing attending school through to a particular grade or earning a diploma; it means that learners learn things about all life and do not just read a particular subject. Lifelong education justifies education in its own right. It may be organized as a series of concrete steps with specific purposes, but it must never stop on the way.

In summary, neither literacy, nor functional literacy, nor basic education, nor lifelong education is effective if it does not succeed in teaching adult learners the newest of human rights – the right to learn!

THINGS TO DO OR THINK ABOUT

1. Is the literacy programme in which you work referred to as 'functional' literacy? Are the teaching of literacy skills and the teaching of economic skills each given due consideration?

2. Does your literacy programme have an 'awareness' component? Is Paulo Freire's 'critical literacy' ever discussed within the programme?

3. Is your literacy programme learner-centred or sponsor-centred? Who decides what literacy is taught?

CHAPTER TWO/SCRAP BOOK

Being literate means participating in a literate society where social functions are controlled by the literate members of the community. (Budd L. Hall, *Past Sectretary-General of the International Council of Adult Education, speaking in Nagoya, Japan, 1990.*)

Literacy is the recapturing of humanity, and this will only be achieved through equal partnership between those who are literate and those who are not. (Taichi Sasaoka and Jun Nishikawa, *Asian Cultural Center for UNESCO, Japan.*)

It is easy to understand how illiteracy not only makes participation in society as a human being difficult, but deprives one of human emtion and culture. 'Literacy' does not mean just attaining the skills of reading and writing; it means regaining human qualities which have been violated. (Lee Wol Soon, *in a paper contributed to the UNESCO symposium organized with the collaboration of Osaka University of Economics and Law; Osaka, Japan, 1-5 July, 1991.*)

The Motivations of Functional Literacy

In the last chapter, many definitions of literacy were presented. Functional literacy was defined as literacy in which literacy and the learning of economic skills is combined into one whole. This definition of functional literacy was later generalized to include awareness. The definition of functionality has now expanded, but economic skills still remain central to the definition of functional literacy.

This emphasis on economic functionality has an important implication. The implication is that economic rewards will be more motivating to adults than other possible motivations. Thus, adults will be more easily attracted to functional literacy classes than to literacy classes that do *not* teach economic skills.

There is some truth in the above suggested connection between economic expectations and learner motivations. For the poor and the deprived, the hope of economic rewards can be highly motivating. That has been found to be generally true.

This is not to say that economic motivations will work for everyone, or that economic motivations will work for someone at all times. Nor are we saying that non-economic motivations do not work with anyone, ever.

Literacy teachers and other grassroots workers must understand the motivational approaches being used in their literacy and development programmes, directly or indirectly. By first understanding the motivational basis of their work themselves, they will be able to explain it to others. More important, they will be able to help individual learners to build upon their existing motivations and acquire new motivations to improve their lives. Teachers will be able to select proper materials and plan curriculum to enable learners to learn.

This chapter's discussion is organized into five sections:

- What are motivations and how are they acquired?
- The priorities among human motivations and what motivates the poor most?
- The triangle of functional literacy: literacy, functionality and awareness
- Writing motivations into literacy materials
- The problems of motivating literacy teachers.

WORDS OF WISDOM AND VOICES FROM THE REAL WORLD

> What kind of people are we?
> We are poor, very poor
> But we are not stupid.
> That is why despite our illiteracy,
> We still exist.
> But we have to know.
> Why should we become literate?
> Can literacy help us live a little better?
> Starve a little less?
> Would it guarantee that the mother and the daughter do
>   not have to share the same sari between them?
> Would it fetch us a newly thatched roof over our heads?
> (From a prose poem by Satyen Moitra, *Bengal Social Service League, Calcutta, India*)

You can not teach anybody anything that he [or she] does not want to learn. (George Sampson)

Our world is a world of mixed motives. (Anonymous)

Motivations are never spontaneous. Motivations have to be mobilized. (The Vice-Minister of Education, Viet Nam, *in a speech at an international literacy seminar, Udaipur, India, 1982*)

When adult learners do not join literacy groups, they are blamed for lack of motivation. When literacy teachers fail to hold classes regularly, they are blamed for lack of motivation. Lack of motivation is the explanation for all and everything that goes wrong or does not happen. This is true for literacy work. This is true for all development work.

When we blame everything on 'lack of motivation', we may actually be showing our 'lack of understanding'. Motivations do not rain from the sky. Motivations are not spontaneous. We need to teach them. For that, we need to understand the nature of human motivations. We need to understand how motivations are acquired. How motivations are taught. How motivations can be sustained.

What are motivations and how are they acquired?

A person is considered to be motivated when he or she is ready to do something without being told to or having to be persuaded. When the motive to learn or to act is already there *in* the person, that person is considered to be motivated.

MOTIVATIONS THAT WE ARE BORN WITH

We are born with some motivations. These motivations are rooted in *biological* needs or in our *felt* needs. We have in-built motivations to satisfy our hunger, our thirst and our sexuality, to escape from pain and to seek comfort.

We are also naturally motivated to seek social interactions with other human beings. We are naturally motivated to explore what happens around us. To be social and to be curious can perhaps be called socio-bio-logical needs. These are felt needs in the real sense.

MOTIVATIONS THAT WE MUST LEARN

But all motivations are not in-built. All needs are not already felt needs. Many needs have to be *fashioned* for the development of individuals and families, and for the progress of communities and nations. Indeed, the most important needs and motivations in our world are learned.

For example, needs to be peaceful, to be democratic, to be educated and to be a civilized member of the community are all fashioned needs. Of course, motivations to fulfil these fashioned needs are learned as well. These motivations are learned from parents, peers, teachers, priests, leaders, writers, and great men and women of history. Motivations are learned through a combination of information and persuasion. Motivations are learned through upbringing and education.

Thus, when adults do not want to learn to read, it is time to teach them a new motivation – the motivation to read. When women with many children do not want to participate in family planning clinics, it is time to teach them a new motivation – the motivation to participate in the family planning clinic.

We must, however, learn to motivate without stigmatization. The battle against illiteracy should not become a battle against the illiterate.

There are cases where hidden illiterates or semi-literates lost their jobs because the literacy workers knowingly or unknowingly exposed them!

In either of the two cases above, we can not simply give up and say: 'Illiterate adults are not motivated to learn to read'; 'These women are not motivated to practise family planning!' We must motivate the mother with many children to participate in the family planning clinic. We must motivate illiterate adults to come to literacy classes.

Development work is not merely selling things to people who are already motivated to buy. Development work requires the creation of new needs, new wants and new motivations. Unfortunately, people do not always know what is in their self-interest. They must be made aware of socially-desirable needs and protected from learning artificial and undesirable needs.

Thus, the first task of the literacy teacher is to help adults to acquire a new motivation – the motivation to become literate. The second task is to help adults actually to learn to read and write. Once the first task is accomplished, then the second will be easy.

To sum up, the sequence in literacy work should always be this: first, motivate; second, teach.

The priorities among human motivations and what motivates the poor most

Human beings have many purposes and many motivations. For example, we are motivated to obtain food. We are motivated to protect our children. We are motivated to attend the wedding of a friend. We are motivated to look for better jobs.

Often human beings have mixed motivations for doing the same one thing. For example, when going to attend the wedding of a friend, we may be motivated also to have some good food and drinks, to meet other friends and to see the new town where the wedding will take place.

Motivations get connected in networks. Good workers often build a new motivation upon already existing motivations. For example, the motivation to join a training course may be built upon the existing motivation to get a better job.

If the gap between an old motivation and a new motivation is too great, a motivational bridge may have to be built. For example, an adult may be motivated to get a better job. The adult may also be motivated to join a training course. But this person may not have the level of literacy to be admitted into the training course. There is an opportunity here to build a motivational bridge between the two existing motivations. Teachers may also face situations where adult learners may have incredibly unrealistic expectations of literacy. In such cases expectations may have to be lowered, without lowering interest in learning.

MOTIVATIONAL PRIORITIES

Human needs are many and we know that we cannot have everything in life. As a result, we arrange our needs by priorities. Then our motivations get arranged according to our needs. These priorities depend upon our stage of life. They also depend on our present conditions.

Some social psychologists have suggested that our needs-motivations can be arranged as a pyramid of priorities. This is not a pyramid that applies to every human being on this globe. Furthermore, as we have indicated above, we do have often mixed motivations. Figure 3.1 demonstrates the pyramid showing the hierarchy of human needs suggested by Professor Maslow, an American psychologist.

Figure 3.1 Maslow's hierarchy of human needs
Computer graphic by Kenichi Kubota, 1991

This pyramid of needs-and-motivations suggests that, under normal conditions, people will first want to take care of their physiological needs of thirst, hunger and rest, and the need to escape pain. Then they would want to take care of the need for safety of themselves and their children.

That is followed by the emotional need to be loved and the social need to be among family and friends, and the community. Then we have a psychological need – the need for self-esteem. We need to feel that we are worth something in life, that we are okay. Finally, we have a kind of spiritual need. It is the need to feel whole, to feel fulfilled.

A literacy worker should be able to see what needs the various participants in his or her class seem to feel most acutely. The literacy teacher then needs to demonstrate how becoming literate and being able to read might help fulfil one, more or all of those needs and how, without literacy, it may be impossible to fulfil those needs. That will help motivate the learners.

WHAT MOTIVATES THE POOR?

To be poor means different things in different countries and different places in the world. In the West, the so-called poor are often better off than the well-off in Africa, Asia or Latin America. This is true at least in terms of material goods.

The poor in developing countries are so poor that new words had to be invented to describe them. They are called the poorest of the poor. The poorest of the poor have nothing. They do not always know from where their next meal is coming. They can carry all their worldly belongings in one basket!

First and foremost, these poorest of the poor have physiological needs. And, therefore, their strongest motivation is to obtain food, clothing and shelter. They need to learn how to obtain food, clothing and shelter. They need to know how to produce more food. They need to know how to store and save food. Since these are the needs they already feel acutely, they are motivated to fulfil these needs. And this is where the needs-motivations of learners connect with the idea of functional literacy. Functional literacy seeks to use the already felt needs of the poor, the existing store of motivations. It does so by teaching economic skills along with literacy – that is, by teaching functional literacy.

THE CONNECTION IS NOT THAT SIMPLE!

There are connections among needs, motivations and functional literacy. However, these connections are not simple.

Adults may ask: Why can't we learn economic skills without having to learn literacy first? Why not save time from literacy and put that time in working on the farm or in the shop? In being productive?

We have to persuade them that learning new things and new ways of doing things without literacy is difficult. We do not have enough extension workers to send one to each and every farmer or worker. But we can send them a copy of a little book or a leaflet on how to grow more or to stay healthy.

We must make non-literates understand that modern ways of doing things cannot be learned and taught orally. People need to be literate to understand lots of things. People need literacy to take notes to be able to remember.

Most important, literacy gives freedom to the farmer and worker to read what he or she needs to read. The farmer will not have to wait to be told by the extension worker. This type of free and independent access to information is important for real development.

Adults may want quick returns and clear-cut results. Even if non-literates are persuaded about the need to become functionally literate, they are often impatient about results. They want quick returns. But stopping land erosion may take months; a crop cycle may involve many months; starting a poultry farm or a small tailoring business takes time; and making money from a business is a long process.

There is another serious matter. Results of functional literacy are not always very clear-cut. Newly literate adults may have learned much about kitchen gardening from the functional literacy class. They may have learned much about good health habits from the functional literacy class. But they do not sit down and count how much money was saved because of the kitchen garden and how much the produce from the kitchen garden contributed to family health. It is difficult to connect learning about good health with savings in medicines and doctor's fees, and with work days added to their working life. These connections are what the literacy teacher will have to enable adult learners to see and be convinced of.

What is promised is not always delivered. Functional literacy projects cannot always teach functionality well enough because the literacy teacher does not have enough functional knowledge.

The literacy teacher may be aware of his or her shortcomings in functional knowledge. But the teacher may have been unable to get extension workers in the field to come and help with functional knowledge and skills.

Even when the teacher and the extension worker are willing to collaborate, there may be no resources in terms of land, seeds, fertilizers or equipment to do effective teaching of functionality or to establish a successful income-generating project. It is unfortunate that sometimes what functional literacy projects promise, they do not deliver.

IN LITERACY WORK, YOU CAN NEVER GO WRONG

Literacy teachers should, of course, do their best in presenting the most effective functional literacy programmes possible. If functional components are not perfect, they should not feel dismayed. There will be at least some functional information in the literacy primer and follow-up books.

Literacy teachers should ensure that participants learn to read and write. If that is ensured, their work will have been a success. In doing literacy work, one can never go wrong.

The triangle of functional literacy: literacy, functionality and awareness

In Chapter 2, we talked about the triangle of functional literacy. We pointed out that literacy work built on the economic function alone has been attacked by some literacy workers who want literacy for empowerment and liberation. Literacy workers, therefore, have added awareness as a third essential component of functional literacy.

Functionality is economic skills, but awareness is wider. It can cover participation in community affairs, exercise of civil rights and responsibilities, and democratization. Awareness may also cover social responsibilities such as sanitation and public health, population, pollution and environment. The triangle of functional literacy is a good idea that deserves a chance to be tried.

It must be pointed out, however, that even with this expanded concept of functional literacy, teachers should be open to additional needs and additional motivations. The general programme may be built around the triangle of functional literacy. But there may be specific needs and specific motivations of individuals in a particular group. For example, in this world of mixed motivations, there may be a mature adult who has spiritual motivations. He or she should be helped to read the scriptures. Another younger man or woman may be interested in enjoying the cultural heritage of the country and may therefore want to read folk tales and epics. Such an individual should be enabled to do so.

In summary, economic skills are central to the programme, but no learner should be denied the opportunity to follow his or her particular motivation or set of mixed motivations.

Writing motivations into literacy materials

Topics of programme development and curriculum development in functional literacy will be discussed later. At that time, we will show how the three components of functional literacy – literacy, functionality and awareness – can be brought together.

At this time, let us state only that the functional component of a functional literacy project is taught through written materials, discussion and practical activities.

The same is true about the teaching of the awareness component of a functional literacy project.

MOTIVATIONAL MESSAGES IN FUNCTIONAL LITERACY MATERIALS

Literacy primers and graded books are *primarily* for teaching reading and writing. As far as possible, the sequence of lessons in these materials follows the logic of language teaching. That is, in a class for teaching English literacy the word 'corn' may have to be taught before teaching the word 'ridges'.

While following the logic of teaching reading and writing, writers of functional literacy materials do include some subject matter content in these materials. There are, however, limits on how much of such information can be included. That is so because the choice and sequencing of words demanded by language teaching is not the same as that demanded by technical teaching.

Two points should be remembered in this regard.

1. Functional literacy primers and graded books can include more motivational material than technical material. The writer will find it relatively easy to inspire a farmer to be a good farmer. To instruct the farmer about the chemistry of pesticides and on how exactly to prepare pesticide solutions will be relatively more difficult to do within the two covers of the primer or a graded book.

2. The second point is that functional literacy materials can never include all that may be necessary for a farmer or a worker to know about an economic activity to generate good income. Practical demonstrations, field visits, experiments and applications will be a necessary part of the overall programme. The learner must be en-

abled to have direct experience through personal involvement in all these functional activities.

The problems of motivating literacy teachers

Literacy teachers, as grassroots workers, are the most important actors in the literacy enterprise. Unfortunately, they are also the most neglected.

Many literacy projects, programmes and campaigns present situations of exploitation. Literacy teachers are often volunteers who are expected to work a few hours every day. They are given a small honorarium. Once appointed, they are expected to do considerable work with learners in the community, before and after the literacy classes, every day, for months and even years.

The expectations are too high in relation to the rewards. Routines get boring. Supervisors and others coming from the headquarters give orders to the literacy teachers. They experience frustrations. There is teacher burn-out!

COLLEGIALITY AND CAPACITATION

There are two very obvious needs. One is the need for collegiality between teachers and others on the literacy team. The supervisor of literacy classes needs to treat the teacher as a colleague. The supervisor should be a friend and mentor to the literacy teacher.

The second important need is capacitation. Few projects, if any, make any training inputs in their teachers. There may be scores of national and provincial seminars every year, but few training camps are organized for supervisors and teachers.

In-service training of teachers should occur regularly. Perhaps there should be training-cum-evaluation camps for teachers from various regions at the end of each and every phase of a literacy project. This will help in the in-service training of teachers and in the evaluation of achievements, and should create a sense of solidarity among teachers.

LITERACY MOTIVATIONS AND LITERACY ENVIRONMENTS

Sometimes literacy workers are told not to waste efforts on motivating people for literacy, not to waste resources on teaching literacy or not to lead people on a road to nowhere. They ask: What is the use of teaching literacy to people when there is no literacy environment? What uses can new literates make of their literacy skills in today's world? These remarks when properly analysed are absurd and the questions raised are naïve.

We should know that there is no place in the world today where the printed word has not reached. There is print in the skies. Printed materials have littered the earth and the ocean beds. There is print on the top of the Mount Everest and I have personally seen printed materials in the middle of the Kalahari desert. No human environment is physically free from print.

Nor is any human environment culturally or symbolically free from print. No longer is there such a thing as an oral society anymore. There are small pre-literate subcultures and illiterate groups and families, but they are not self-contained in their orality. They are submerged in the world of print and have become, by definition, disadvantaged.

Every institution in today's world, everywhere in the world is based on assumptions of literacy. This is true of sacred institutions such as churches and mosques. This is true of secular institutions which collect revenues and assure law and order.

Why should we then not motivate people to become literate? Why should we not help them overcome their disadvantage?

We must also remember that literate environments do not come into being independently of literacy promotion. Literate environments are created by doing literacy work. They are created by helping people to use literacy in their economic, social and political lives. Until all those opportunities arise, people must be enabled to change their lives in personal terms.

THINGS TO DO OR THINK ABOUT

1. Have you been able to discover the felt needs and existing motivations of adult learners in your group? Describe them.

2. Have you done any motivational work in connection with the opening of the class that you now teach? What was your general message? Did it work? What else worked? What did not work?

3. Do you agree with the statement that motivating adults in a literacy class may be like a doctor writing individual prescriptions in a health clinic? Each learner may have to be enabled to develop his or her own motivational mix.

CHAPTER THREE/SCRAP BOOK

The accurate conveyance and dissemination of knowledge is of vital importance, but the low rate of literacy is an enormous obstacle which makes these activities difficult. Health care and development workers are dealing, more or less, with teaching reading and writing. (Dr. Hiromi Kawahara, *Executive Director of Asia Health Institute*)

A great number of mothers I met there were frustrated by their illiteracy, and lamented not being able to absorb even the most basic information.

The situation led to the opening of literacy classes, and I was deeply impressed by the commitment and enthusiasm brought to it by its locally trained leaders. Radios, televisions, and oral communications are not enough; literacy is vital also in the field of health care, and it is the mothers who should be given the top priority. (Dr. Shin Isomura, *Director, Aichi Prefectural Institute of Public Health*)

The State of Kerala [in India] has the highest literacy rate for both men and women. It also has the lowest infant mortality rate, the lowest proportion of married families in the age group 15–19, and very low death rate. Literacy of parents has also produced a very good impact on environment for universal primary education and retention of children in schools. (L. Mishra, *Director–General, National Literacy Mission of the Government of India, in a paper submitted to the Unesco Symposium on the organization of literacy programmes, Osaka, Japan, 1–5 July 1991*)

Chapter Four

Curriculum Development and Programmme Development

To teach literacy as part of a public mission, several questions need to be answered. What should be the language of literacy? What should be the level of literacy and numeracy? What economic skills should be taught? What should be taught to promote awareness? How should all these content areas be integrated into an overall curriculum?

In addition, there are a series of questions about programme development. Who should teach what, to whom, when and in what settings? What should be the organization? Who should control what?

WHY SHOULD TEACHERS KNOW?

If the curriculum development and the programme development are both done at higher levels, why do we have to include a discussion of curriculum development and programme development in this *Sourcebook* for teachers and other workers at the grassroots? There are two reasons.

Workers at the grassroots level need to have some basic ideas about curriculum development and programme development. Only then will they be able to understand why project organizers at the higher levels have asked them to follow a particular curriculum. They will also understand the reason why the programme is organized the way it is. Their everyday work will make better sense to them.

The second reason is that curriculum development and programme development done at higher levels are *never* complete. All the personal learning needs of individuals can never be anticipated by the curriculum developers from above. All the learning needs of communities can not be anticipated before hand. Learning emergencies also arise! If there is a cholera outbreak, the literacy teacher must immediately add the topic of 'precautions against cholera' to the curriculum. To do this the teacher must understand the big picture of curriculum and programme development. Only then he or she will be able to merge the new local curriculum into the one already developed by specialists at the levels above. Only then will the grassroots workers be able to make the necessary additions or adaptations. Local adaptations work wonders. Good grassroots workers always make local adaptations.

This chapter is divided into seven sections; the first of four deal with curriculum development and the last three with programme development.

- Three major curriculum components of functional literacy
- Weaving together the various curriculum threads
- Opening up the curriculum: expanding the meanings of functionality; reflecting local needs
- Role of testing in curriculum development
- Designing instructional roles and ways of co-operating
- Modes of mobilization and programme boundaries
- Technical support, local support, administration and supervision.

WORDS OF WISDOM AND VOICES FROM THE REAL WORLD

We don't get a square meal
We have few clothes
We don't have proper shelter
And to top it all, floods come and wash away everything.
Then comes a long spell of drought drying up everything.
Would it help if we became literate?
We are weak and ill very often.
Will the programme teach us
How to take care of our health, and become strong?
If it does, then we will come.
Would literacy help us know the laws that have changed the status of women?
And the laws that protect the tribals among us?
Would it help us know how to raise our yield, and increase our income?
And from where we could borrow money on easy terms, and what benefits would we get from the cooperatives?
Would we get better seeds, fertilizer and all the water we need?

Would we get proper wages?
And this we think is learning for living.
(From a prose poem by Satyen Moitra, *Bengal Social Service League, Calcutta, India*)

If you educate a man you educate a person, but if you educate a woman you educate a family. (Ruby Manikan, *an Indian Church Leader*)

'Several people in the village used to tease us, being the only women in our literacy class, saying, "You are women. Why do you need to know how to read and write?" Many laughed at us but we kept on learning. Now I have benefited from being persistent and ignoring those jeering men and my life is better for it'. This young tribal woman is now the leader of a Child-feeding Centre... Her testimony is only one example of how literacy is transforming a tribal community in India. (From the Summer Institute of Linguistics *Annual Report*, 1990)

In this chapter, we discuss curriculum development and programme development. The two processes are directly inter-linked with each other.

What is curriculum? Curriculum is everything that is envisioned to be taught and learned within an educational programme. Curriculum is the sum of all reading, writing and discussing in the class. Curriculum is all the demonstrating and viewing and doing as part of learning skills. Curriculum is participation in all the social and cultural and political activities that teachers and learners go through.

What is curriculum development? Curriculum development means making curricular plans and curriculum choices. This is what gets put on paper. What will be read and at what level? What will be written? What demonstrations will be made? What field activities will be followed? Curriculum development is typically done at higher levels of literacy projects, programmes or campaigns.

What is programme development? Once the general outlines of a curriculum have been developed, then the next step is programme development. Curriculum plans have to be shared, curriculum materials have to be delivered and the curriculum has to be brought alive in the lives of learners and teachers. Practical plans for the delivery of instruction constitute programme development. Like curriculum development, programme development also is done at higher levels of literacy projects, programmes or campaigns.

Three major curriculum components of functional literacy

As we have indicated before, economics is the major focus of functional literacy. However, awareness is also an essential part of functional literacy as practised today. Thus, functional literacy today contains three curriculum components: literacy, functionality and awareness.

Literacy. Literacy is the ability to read and write in a chosen language of literacy. Choice of the language of literacy may have been decided upon for cultural reasons, economic reasons or political reasons. Each literacy project, programme, or campaign needs to develop an operational definition of literacy (see the *operational* definition of literacy developed within the Indian literacy programme, Chapter 2, pp. 35–36).

Sustainable literacy. There are limits to our freedom to define literacy. We cannot, for example, define literacy merely as the ability to sign one's name. That will be quite unsatisfactory. The definition of literacy should be of a standard high enough that it becomes sustainable. In other words, it should be of a standard that helps in retention of the literacy skills once acquired. The new literate should not relapse into illiteracy. A literacy level roughly equivalent to the fourth grade of the school is considered retainable and, therefore, sustainable. Creating conditions in which new literates can put their literacy to use in their daily lives will further help sustainability.

Language of literacy. The choice of the language of literacy is a question of policy, curriculum and methodology at the same time.

If literacy is taught in the mother tongue, there will be the problem of handling the transition from mother tongue literacy to literacy in the official or the national language.

If literacy is being taught in the official or national language, which is not necessarily spoken by adults, the problem is not that of teaching literacy *but that of teaching literacy in a second language.*

The writing curriculum in literacy. Literacy is the ability to read *and* write. Writing is an important part of literacy. Unfortunately, curricular questions about writing do not get the attention they deserve.

There are a few literacy workers who suggest that emphasis in literacy teaching should be on the teaching of reading, not writing. They point out to the fact that it is possible to teach reading without having to teach writing at the same time. They say that reading is much more frequently used in real life than is writing. They also think that the teaching of writing slows the learner's progress in a literacy programme. For all these reasons they think reading should be taught first and writing – maybe – later. Not everyone considers this to be good advice.

Most literacy workers want to include both reading and writing in the curriculum and teach the two together. In the process of teaching, they suggest, the processes of reading and writing support each other. They point out that while writing may not be as frequent as reading in the life of new literates, it is equally significant.

The significance of writing in the curriculum of literacy lies in the fact that it enables the new learner to write about his or her own world – write names, memories, songs, beliefs, ideas and personal knowledge.

Writing curriculum in exemplary literacy programmes does not stop at penmanship but goes to the extent of helping the adult learner claim a voice and discover what he or she thinks.

Numeracy curriculum in literacy. Numeracy is rarely a part of the popular definition of literacy. Fortunately, this serious omission is fixed during the process of curriculum development. There is hardly a curriculum for literacy that does not include some numeracy.

Definition of numeracy. Numeracy has been defined as the ability to understand and use mathematics as a means of communication. The numerate should be able to understand a situation described to him or her in numbers and other mathematical terms, should be able to describe a situation in mathematical terms and should be able to use mathematical symbols to find answers to numerical questions.

Mathematics in traditional cultures. The highly technical definition of numeracy above should not dismay the literacy worker. Numeracy is not something beyond the capacity of common folk living in rural areas and urban slums. Indeed, all societies have incorporated mathematics into their traditional cultures. And most adults who come to learn to read already have some level of numeracy.

Mathematics educator A. J. Bishop argues that there are six fundamental mathematical activities which are both universal, in that they appear to be carried out by every cultural group ever studied, and also necessary and sufficient for the development of mathematical knowledge. These six activities are:

1. Counting: This may involve tallying; or using objects like shells, or seeds; or using knots on string to record; or having special number-words or names.

2. Locating: Locating is also a mathematical skill. It involves exploring spatial environment with diagrams or drawings or words to fix locations.

3. Measuring: This skills involves quantitative comparisons using objects or tokens; and having associated measuring-words or units.

4. Designing: This involves creating shapes or designs for an object or for a part of the environment. This may result in a concrete object or a mental view.

5. Playing: The mathematics in playing is involved as formalized rules for playing those games are devised.

6. Explaining: This involves finding ways to account for the existence of various phenomena.

The challenge in developing curriculum for numeracy, therefore, involves determining the needs for numeracy within the fast-changing socio-economic contexts of learners, building new mathematical skills on the old mathematical skills already known to adult learners and teaching the conventions whereby oral mathematics can be written down on paper so that various formal operations can be performed.

A numeracy curriculum to adapt from. The International Conference on Developing Mathematics in the Third World Countries (Khartoum, 1979) agreed on the following goals for mathematics education in primary schools. These apply also to adults bypassed by the formal system:

1. Functional numeracy (including an understanding of place value, decimals and fractions, and an appreciation of the size of the number). Functional implies not only knowing *how* but also knowing *when* to perform an arithmetical operation.

2. Acquisition of certain mental attitudes to enable the development of problem-solving strategies.

3. Acquisition of techniques of representing and interpreting data (numerical and otherwise).

4. Measurement and approximation. (Note the inclusion of approximation – the ability to make guesses with reasonable correctness.)

5. Development of spatial concepts and the ability to represent them (e.g., scale drawing, maps).

One should note that there is a big overlap of skills between what is expected to be in the culture already and what is new that is to be taught.

Functionality has come to mean knowledge and skills of production that can be applied to generate income in rural or urban settings. In rural areas it typically means agricultural skills and related economic skills such as poultry farming, fish farming and cattle raising. Craft work for men and women is also a popular income-generating activity.

Some functional literacy projects may teach agro-industrial skills such as furniture making for use in the community, making home appliances such as modern fuel-efficient ovens, repairing and maintaining agricultural tools, producing fuel substitutes from sawdust and other organic materials.

Good functional literacy curricula do not simply teach methods of doing things; they also teach the science on which those economic skills are based as well as management skills.

Scientific basis of production. One can not teach *all* science to adults within a year or less of a literacy course. The main idea here is that adults should not simply be given instructions to follow certain production procedures on the farm or in the factory. They should be explained the reason 'Why?'.

That will make it possible for them to apply the principles learned in one setting to another setting. What they learned about the use of pesticides in their fields, they should be able to apply to the use of medicines obtained for the family. What they learned about pollution in the factory, they should be able to transfer to the problems of pollution in their homes and neighbourhoods.

Management of income-generating activities. The teaching of management skills is becoming an important part of the curriculum in functional literacy skills. Leadership and participation in income generating activities requires basic knowledge about planning, banking, accounting, purchasing, storing, marketing and selling. These skills are required whether the income-generating activity is a village bakery that sells bread within the village or a little silk-weaving co-operative that exports its production to foreign markets.

Fruits of functionality. In case of the subsistence farmer and the self-employed, the fruits of functionality will go to the individual new literate. This is not always so for those who are wage earners in large agricultural estates, mines and factories. There the organizers of functional literacy will have to ensure that the fruits of functionality are equitably divided among all concerned – the workers, management and the proprietors.

Expanded concept of functionality. In some recent UNESCO documents functionality is seen to consist of four parts: socio-political skills, life skills, work and occupational skills, and cultural development.

Socio-political skills should ensure full participation in community life. The new literate should be enabled to exercise his or her civic rights and responsibilities. The relationship between literacy and democracy should become clear. The ethical necessity of literacy as a human right should become clear as well.

Life skills should teach the new literate to be health conscious and to be sensitive to personal cleanliness and sanitation in the surroundings at home and at work. The new literate should be able to learn skills to take care of the family and of the environment.

The work and occupational skills should enable the adult to make a living and provide for the family at an adequate level. Finally, the newly literate adult should be able to enjoy culture and contribute to its growth and renewal.

AWARENESS

The curriculum component of awareness seeks to make people aware of both their rights and their responsibilities as citizens. It is not easy to design a good awareness curriculum. That is so because an awareness curriculum raises political questions which some governments do not want to be raised.

Yet there is a considerable part of the curriculum of awareness that is not controversial. Awareness of human rights, awareness of the need to participate in the community, concern about unemployment, environment, deforestation, pollution, AIDS and world peace are all important issues today for the awareness curriculum. (Please note that there is some overlap between the functionality curriculum and awareness curriculum.)

Example one: curriculum content of awareness. Many different things have been suggested for inclusion in the awareness curriculum in UNESCO documents.

- Fundamental rights as enshrined in the country's constitution (should know at least that the bureaucrats are not the common people's masters but public servants).

- Race relations, casteism.
- Peace, bringing out the role of the world industrial complex in making wars and how the poor die in the nation's wars.
- Media control. Who controls media and to what purpose?
- Women's issues.
- Environment, and how some people exploit the environment as free and how the poor might be paying the highest costs for the destruction of the environment.
- Family planning. Control of women's bodies.
- Development ethics.

Example two: a view from Japan. A manual published by the National Federation of UNESCO Associations in Japan in support of their UNESCO Co-Action Learning Centre Programme expands the definition as follows:

'Awareness Raising is most critical to combat the vicious cycle of poverty, disease, conflict, powerlessness and illiteracy among people. This is essential for people in least industrialized societies as well as most industrialized societies. Learning Centers should organize programmes in Awareness Raising so that individuals, families, groups and communities begin to understand the causes that make people happy or unhappy, progress or degenerate, peaceful or violent. It is this understanding that leads human beings to right action. True awareness of oneself, one's family, the community, the broader society, nature and environment is the key to real self-development leading to peace, contentment and happiness.'

Example three: awareness as information-that-matters. In Papua New Guinea, literacy and awareness are claimed to have been combined directly both conceptually and organizationally. There is a literacy and awareness secretariat within the government.

Awareness campaigns conducted by the government seek to 'help people understand the changes that are occurring in contemporary society'. Themes of awareness differ as different cultural, social and economic needs arise, covering: law and order, national unity, substance abuse, land mobilization, census, election procedures and so on.

ASSESSMENT OF LEARNERS NEEDS

An assessment of the needs of learners is an essential part of curriculum development. Needs assessment typically involves going to the learners themselves and asking them about their needs. Even when curriculum planners think that they already know people's needs, they should still do needs assessment of some kind. It is sure to teach them new things about adults they want to serve. At the very least needs assessments will prove the truthfulness of the lists of needs planners already have developed.

<u>GENERATING CURRICULUM ACTIVITIES</u>

The grid shown in Table 4.1 can be used to generate items for a functional literacy curriculum.

Table 4.1

	Literacy	Functionality	Awareness
Knowledge	?	?	?
Attitudes	?	?	?
Performance skills	?	?	?

Using the grid. One should use the grid above as a device to generate curricular items. Separate lists may be made for knowledge, attitudes and skills to be included in the functional literacy curriculum.

In doing so, one will have to think from two to three different perspectives at the same time.

1. One will have to keep in mind the needs generated during the needs assessment exercise.

2. One will have to put in items that seem obviously necessary to round off the curriculum.

3. One will have to keep in mind the objectives of the functional literacy programme so that the level of content chosen is appropriate.

The various items generated by the grid should be clustered together and put in a proper sequence.

Weaving together the various curriculum threads

The technical phrase for the weaving together of diverse curriculum threads is 'curricular integration'.

In an ideal functional literacy programme literacy and functionality are integrated perfectly. The weaving together of the two is so good that the learner is aware of learning one thing, not two. The learner does not experience literacy and functionality separately. The learner experiences just one thing – functional literacy.

Such integration is not easy to achieve. In fact, it is much easier said than done. When we add awareness to the functional literacy curriculum, things become even more difficult. Why is this so?

THE CLASH BETWEEN THE LOGICAL SEQUENCE OF LANGUAGE
AND THE LOGICAL SEQUENCE OF SUBJECT MATTER

Integration of literacy and functionality (and then of awareness) is difficult because of a logical clash. This is the clash between on the one hand the logic and therefore the sequence of language teaching, and on the other hand the logic and therefore the sequence of subject matter of functionality and awareness.

The teaching of language does not have to use the alphabetic method. However, the logic of teaching languages has to be respected. There has to be a particular sequence in which words and sentences are introduced in language teaching. Simple words must come first, longer and complex words may come later. Concrete words must come first, abstract words may come later. Most frequently used words must come first, less frequently used words may come later.

The teaching of subject matter must also respect the logic and, therefore, the sequence of teaching subject matter. Some basic ideas from introductory physics of heat and light must be taught first. Only then can one teach how to design and build fuel-efficient ovens for the kitchen or solar heaters for water. Some basic ideas from animal biology must be taught before teaching poultry farming. Some simple principles of chemistry must be taught before teaching proper use of pesticides.

The language sequences for literacy teaching and subject matter sequences for teaching functionality (or awareness) are *not* the same. That is where the clash is. That is what makes integration so difficult.

Since the two logics (of literacy and of functionality) are not the same, less than perfect solutions have to be invented. We suggest two ways of integration: programmatic integration and organic/thematic integration.

We suggest also that in phase one of a literacy programme, only programmatic integration is possible. In phase two of a literacy programme, an organic/thematic integration also becomes possible (see Table 4.2).

Table 4.2. Possible solutions to curricular integration

	First phase: 'Learning to read'	Second phase: 'Reading to learn'
Programmatic integration	X	
Organic/ thematic integration		X

Programmatic integration. By programmatic integration, we mean integration through programme organization. That is, literacy, functionality and awareness are taught as two or three separate streams. But integration is achieved by teaching all this material to the same group of learners. The literacy teacher, the political education teacher and the extension worker teach as a team. They make continuous cross-references to the three kinds of materials. This is the only reasonable kind of integration possible in the first phase of literacy teaching, the learning-to-read phase.

Organic/thematic integration. A more organic integration by themes is possible during the second phase of literacy, that is, the reading-to-learn phase. By now participants will have learned to read and genuine integration of language and subject matter will be possible.

Thus, in phase one, the learners 'learn to read'. In phase two, the learners 'read to learn' – that is, to use their skills in the 3-Rs in learning economic functionality and issues of awareness.

Opening up the curriculum: expanding the meaning of functionality and reflecting local needs

As we have indicated, the concept of functional literacy as proposed at the 1965 UNESCO Conference in Tehran included primarily literacy and economic function. The concept was attacked for its *exclusive* focus on economic functions. It had to be expanded to include awareness.

Today, there is an acceptance of the motivational role of the economic function in literacy in the Third World countries. At the same time, there is considerable pressure towards expanding the concept of functional literacy to include more than economic functionality.

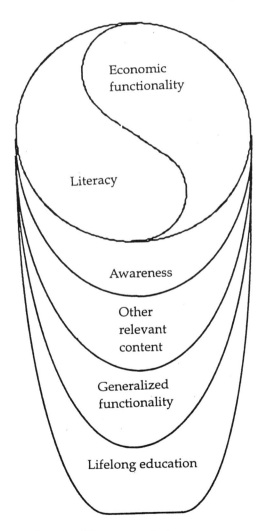

Figure 4.1 Visualizing functional literacy curriculum
Computer graphic by Kenichi Kubota, 1991

The suggestion is made to include in the concept of functionality any function that learners may want to assign to their literacy skills including human rights and spiritual and religious needs (Figure 4.1).

HOW DOES THE LITERACY TEACHER REFLECT LOCAL NEEDS IN THE FUNCTIONAL LITERACY CURRICULUM?

There is an important demand on functional literacy curricula to include teaching to meet local learning needs of communities. These needs may be economic, social, political and cultural.

We do not expect the literacy teacher to be competing with the curriculum development specialists working at the upper levels of the programme. Nor do we expect the teacher to do major curriculum development at the field level. But the teacher will be expected to do 'small' curriculum development. In other words, the teacher will be expected to be adapting and adding to the curriculum as he or she works with learners.

Adapting general functional literacy to local needs. The literacy teacher should begin with his or her own learner group. The teacher should ask the learners if curriculum already designed for them is relevant. If it needs adaptations, what kinds of things would the learners want to be changed or added. Do the learners need to learn about things not discussed within the curriculum?

If additions and adaptations are necessary, then the problem of teaching those new things must be addressed. Also, there will be the problem of obtaining materials for teaching. However, even a well-qualified and experienced teacher should *not* try to do everything by himself or herself. In these adaptations and additions in regard to the curriculum, the teacher should be an organizer, a manager, a midwife and a broker *all at the same time.*

The teacher should bring together those who want to learn and those who have knowledge to impart. The teacher should explore where one might find materials for teaching locally-relevant knowledge and activities. The teacher should get those materials for the learners. Most of the time, the extension workers already working in the field will be the greatest resource for local adaptations of curriculum.

Role of testing in curriculum development

Curriculum development includes not only teaching but also testing. Curriculum is designed in terms of particular objectives and needs. It lists knowledge content, attitudes and performance of skills. One needs to find out if objectives were accomplished at an acceptable level.

Testing of achievement is necessary. But the purpose and style of testing adults in functional literacy groups should not be the same as testing in schools. Testing of adults should be diagnostic – to find out what adults are learning, what some adults have not yet learned and why.

Testing of adults should be as far as possible 'invisible'; it should be built into the materials and the routines of teaching and learning so that it is viewed not as a examination but rather as feedback useful for learning.

Testing of adults should be participative. That is, adults should take part in their own testing. For example, adults may write tests for each other, devise testing games, and mark their own tests and determine their own criteria of success.

SELF-TESTING BY LEARNERS

Everyone talks of self-testing, but few are able to use it for themselves or their learners. It is easier said than done. One can informally ask an adult learner how he or she thinks he is doing? One could ask learners if they are satisfied with what they are learning? This, however, may give us nothing more than a sense of their 'personal feelings'. More useful information of this kind is hard to get. It takes professionally trained evaluators, time and effort, and money.

One example is the Center for Literacy in Philadelphia (United States) which uses teacher-learner planning conferences during the intake session. These conferences are repeated every six months for assessment. Items such as the learner's everyday life, reading and writing strategies, interests, perceptions of reading and writing, and goals are considered. A portfolio of the learner's accomplishments and current work is kept. Success is measured in terms of the learner's own goals.

Advantages of such evaluation are obvious. The instructor is the direct beneficiary of this knowledge. It emphasizes what the learner can and cannot do. There is an opportunity to motivate the learner in terms of his or her personal goals. There is no test anxiety, that is, the fear of examinations is reduced. Since it is a mutual affair, the learner is actively involved and gains respect for himself or herself. It is worth emulating these strategies.

Designing instructional roles and ways of co-operating

Programme development involves many elements. One such element is developing roles and designations. Job cards have to be developed for each role-designation. Many questions need to be answered. Should there be a separate literacy teacher? Should literacy teachers be full-time or part-time? Should they be paid or should they be volunteers? Should the primary school teacher be asked to teach a class of adult literacy in the evening? Should extension workers teach literacy classes?

Functional literacy is not a one-person job. Co-operation between different departments – agriculture, health, family planning and labour – is necessary. This co-operation has to be both formal and informal. Formal arrangements are necessary but not enough. In the same way, informal arrangements among workers in the field are necessary, but not enough.

Co-operation is more than exchanging greetings or attending each other's functions, or coming to teach or demonstrate if requested. Co-operation means that local planning should be done co-operatively. It means that local resources from different sources are shared to avoid overlap and maximize their usefulness.

Modes of mobilization and programme boundaries

Programme development also must decide upon the ways of mobilization of people and organization of functional literacy initiatives.

Typical modes of organization-mobilization are: project, programme and campaign. As indicated earlier, projects are specific to particular client groups or institutions, programmes are large-scale initiatives but typically controlled by the government and campaigns typically involve the masses.

It is also necessary to draw boundaries of literacy work at the local level. Questions such as What villages? What occupational or age groups? What number? Selected on what criteria? need answers.

PROGRAMME BOUNDARIES

Programme development may involve questions of focus by constituencies, regions, age-groups and the like. Programmes may be rural or urban or both. Programmes may be gender-based, focusing on the interests of women.

Programmes may pay special attention to particular disadvantaged groups such as women, early school-leavers, out-of-school youth, language minorities, migrant workers, rural immigrants to the urban areas, urban poor, rural poor, economic and political refugees and the incarcerated. For example, functional literacy projects often select particular occupational groups in the so-called productive age of 15–35 or 15–45 depending on the country. These programme choices are not technical; they have serious social and political consequences.

Technical support, local support, administration and supervision

Programme development also has to take care of the needs of technical support and local support, and plan for administration and supervision of work at the grassroots level.

Technical support. Literacy work needs technical support from scholars inside and outside universities and specialized institutions. Sometimes such technical support may come from outside the country. There is need for vocabulary research. There is need of people who can write materials, and train teachers and supervisors. There is need of people who can write tests and make evaluation plans.

Local support. Literacy work seldom succeeds without local support. It can be easily subverted, if local support is not available. Programme developers must take in view this aspect of programme development. This generally means bringing in popular leaders in the area to enthuse local leaders and people. After the visit, there should be collaboration and participation with local leaders for continued local support.

Administration. Organizations of literacy should be 'enabling' organizations, that is, they should enable local leaders, literacy teachers, extension workers and learners to do the things that need to be done. They should not think of administering their work and controlling their lives but rather of providing them all the possible back-up support and service. Then they would have helped them to work effectively.

Supervision. It follows that the role of a supervisor in functional literacy will be that of a mentor, a helpful colleague and not as one who comes to the field to investigate and to order teachers around.

FUNCTIONAL LITERACY CURRICULUM AND PROGRAMME: THE CASE OF INDONESIA

Curriculum development and programme development are often mixed up in real-life situations. An example of nonformal basic education (which equals functional literacy) in Indonesia is described below very briefly to demonstrate how an actual programme has been shaped. The various components of the programme are presented here.

Kejar Pekat A. This element of the programme is implemented at the village level. It is designed for illiterates – adults and dropouts from the elementary schools. Learner groups consist of five to ten people. They use materials in the form of sheets and booklets, A1 to A100, called Kejar Pekat A. Successful completion of Kejar Pekat A is considered equivalent to elementary education.

Kejar Usaha. Kejar Usaha is the name for Income Generating Learning Groups. These groups consist of three to ten members and typically function at the village level. Those admitted have completed Kejar Pekat A. Dropouts from the junior and senior high schools, and sometimes even from the universities also join the programme. The government gives grants to be used as a revolving fund.

Apprenticeship programme. The programme operates at village as well as sub-district levels. It has been developed essentially for dropouts from the junior and senior high schools. Kejar Pekat A graduates and university dropouts also join in.

The government gives a grant to the apprenticeship centre for each member actually enrolled as apprentice. A village carpenter shop, for example, could become such an apprenticeship centre.

Private nonformal adult education for adults. These private enterprises operate at all levels – village, sub-district and district. They cover all comers from new literates and semi-literates to university students. Students pay fees for the privilege of attending classes.

Kejar Pekat B. This Pekat is new and is still on trial in the field. Successful completion is considered equivalent to junior high school.

This Pekat is also integrated with income-generating activities. Learners get together in groups of five to twenty. Priority is given to age-group 12 to 25.

As can be seen, the Indonesian functional literacy curriculum is carefully graded. While Kejar Pekat B curriculum does provide opportunities to acquire skills and to earn an income, it is, at the same time, organized to be equivalent to junior high school diploma.

The curriculum and programme development of functional literacy in Thailand developed three programmes: literacy and basic education, skills training, and news and information.

Equivalences between grade levels have been built carefully between formal schooling and functional literacy (which is the same thing as nonformal basic education). For example, the initial literacy course which teaches a vocabulary of 200 words in three months is equivalent to Grade 2 of elementary school. The functional literacy course that teaches a vocabulary of 500 words in five months is equivalent to Grade 4 of elementary school. Skills training, and news and information are part of both these courses.

Thailand has introduced a very interesting way of making curriculum relevant to regional and local needs. This is done as follows: 60 per cent of the curriculum is considered core curriculum and is taught everywhere in the country; 20 per cent of the curriculum must reflect regional content and is developed in the region; and the last 20 per cent of the curriculum must reflect local content and is meant to be developed locally.

FUNCTIONAL LITERACY PROGRAMME IN MALI, WEST AFRICA

Both of the above examples are from Asia. A continent away in Africa there is another interesting example of how curriculum development and programme development interact to produce a programme on the ground.

The programme in Mali includes both functional literacy and post-literacy aspects aimed primarily at rural youth and adults. Literacy is taught in national languages and includes numeracy as an important component.

Short courses may be of forty-five days or less. Longer courses last from five to six months. These courses are run by animators (instructional leaders) from the villages or literacy agents from the outside. The teaching methodology is that of group learning.

Post-literacy courses seek to serve the individual, the family and the community by providing knowledge and skills. The content covered is agriculture, animal husbandry, health, technology and management. Note that learning of functional knowledge is not the same thing as income-generating activities – a distinction is made between them. The courses are conducted generally by trained technicians and occasionally by village animators. Learning methodology is once again that of group learning.

Popular literacy education programmes are most commonly associated with Latin America and most owe their inspiration to the work of Paulo Freire, the world-renowned Brazilian philosopher and educator.

Popular literacy education programmes are programmes organized in the people's interest. These programmes are nested within programmes of community organization. The overall objective is the political transformation of oppressed societies.

These programmes do not have a curriculum and a programme system in the sense of examples described above. They both emerge through participative actions within community. Some version of the Freirian method is used in this process.

The Freirian method involves at least the following general steps:

1. A team of committed and concerned individuals acquaints itself with the community.

2. The team delimits the area of action geographically – even though, culturally speaking, there are no boundaries.

3. The team establishes contact with *all* possible people in the community, including leaders in official and popular institutions.

4. The team identifies a group of people interested in learning literacy. There is a shared understanding from the very beginning that in 'reading the word' they will be learning to 'read the world'.

5. In genuine dialogue with each other, a thematic analysis of problem is conducted. Justice, education, government and industry are all discussed. In most cases, illustrations are used to stimulate discussion.

6. A particular theme is chosen for codification in the people's language.

7. In a process of critical analysis, reading the word and reading the world are combined.

8. Dialogic action leads to praxis, that is, action will be planned and undertaken to transform oppressive reality.

THINGS TO DO OR THINK ABOUT

1. What are the curricular needs of your group of learners that are not being met by the 'official' curriculum of the literacy programme? What are you planning to do about it?

2. Have you considered adding some uniquely local curriculum to your class? What is it? Do you have the knowledge or the know-how to deliver this part of the curriculum? Is there anyone in the community or nearby who can help? Can extension workers working in the field help? Will you be able to prepare instructional materials to teach that part of the curriculum? Can learners in the class themselves help?

3. Is there a proper balance between central control and local initiative in your literacy programme? If you are not satisfied, what needs to happen?

4. Are there some community resources that have not been used in programme planning? For example, is there a retired school teacher or a military person who could make particular contributions? Do you think school children are able to teach their parents at home?

Chapter Five

What do we know about the Teaching of Reading, Writing, Numeracy and Functional Skills?

Now we must move to concrete questions of clear and direct interest to workers at the grassroots. What is the best method of teaching reading? What is the best method of teaching writing? Should reading and writing be taught together? What is the best method of teaching numeracy? Can the 3 R's (reading, writing and arithmetic) be taught together, as one?

What is the best way for teaching functionality – particularly functionality in economic skills? Can functionality and literacy be taught together? How? How can learning of economic skills be changed into real income-generating activities?

What is the real meaning of awareness? How does one teach awareness? How does the teacher himself or herself acquire awareness to be able to create it among adult learners? In this chapter, we will answer these various questions.

Literacy teachers and extension workers are the primary users of the methods we talk about in this chapter. If they do not know what methods to use, we are all in trouble. If they do not understand why they are being asked to use those methods, they will never be able to adapt to the learning needs of their learners. They will not be able to invent new solutions. The special needs of adults in their groups will then not be fully served.

This chapter is organized into seven sections:

- The method of functional literacy in the context of adult education
- General methods of teaching literacy
- General methods of teaching writing
- General methods of teaching numeracy

- Methods of integrating the 3 R's into the teaching of functional literacy
- Integrating the teaching of functional skills with the teaching of literacy
- Promoting awareness

WORDS OF WISDOM AND VOICES FROM THE REAL WORLD

Reading maketh a full man; conference a ready man; and writing an exact man. (Francis Bacon)

Without writing, we should still be in the Stone Age. Without writing, the darkness would be darker, and our worries more worrying. Writing is essentially a human activity. Being able to read and write gives us greater hope, an extra chance. (Haroun Tazieff in *Letters of Life*, Nathan/UNESCO, 1991)

Literacy to be meaningful must begin with a critical understanding of self and a searching examination of social, economic and cultural realities. The relationship which matters in literacy, meaningfully defined, is not that between the eye and the page, but that between the critical faculty of the mind and the complexities of the world. (Paulo Freire in *Letters of Life*, Nathan/UNESCO, 1991)

You have heard the phrase 'teaching method' many times. You may have heard it during training from your supervisor or from other literacy teachers or colleagues. As part of your training, you must have been given very specific instructions on methods of teaching reading and writing in your particular project. Those are the instructions you should continue to follow as you work with your adult learners in classes and groups. We are not asking you to reject or abandon the instructions you may have received from your trainers about the use of instructional materials in your particular project. What we seek to do is to provide a general background to methods of teaching literacy, functionality and awareness. Thus, this chapter is about the general methodology of teaching literacy; it brings out general principles and procedures hidden in concrete methods of teaching literacy as well as what is unique to each of the methods of teaching literacy.

Once we know what is general and what is specific in each of the methods of teaching literacy, we will be able to choose among the methods to suit our values and our circumstances at the project level. If a set of methods has already been adopted, we will understand its working and be able to use it more effectively.

Let us remember that methods are important both for the teacher and the learner. But let us remember also that for the highly-motivated learner, methods become marginal. Highly-motivated learners can learn to read without the teacher, without any special learning materials and without the benefit of any particular method. I have personally come in contact with some such learners during my working life as a literacy worker in various places in the world, over the years. However, for most learners, most of the time, using a systematic method helps a lot.

The method of functional literacy in the context of adult education

Earlier in this *Sourcebook*, functional literacy was defined to include three components – literacy, functionality and awareness.

An objective of functional literacy is, of course, to enable adult learners to function effectively in their societies. Another objective is to continue learning, to stay functional in societies that are ever-changing. All societies are becoming print cultures. Hence our emphasis on literacy and print.

THE METHODOLOGY OF ADULT EDUCATION

Think further about the objectives and components of functional literacy in the two paragraphs above. These are also the objectives and components of adult education in most parts of the world. Indeed, functional literacy workers are advised to conduct their work first within the context of adult education and then within the larger context of lifelong education.

In providing functional literacy, the methodology of adult education should always be respected. Let us quickly remind ourselves of the spirit of the methodology of adult education.

Respect for the learner. First and foremost, literacy teachers of adults must respect their learners. Genuine respect is, of course, more than mere politeness.

Literacy teachers must accept the fact that their learners all have had long and significant experiences during their lives. In raising their families and in earning a living, they have learned a lot about the ways of the world. All have rich life-experience and some real wisdom. They deserve respect even though they may not yet be able to read and write.

Participative learning. In a learning group of adults, participative learning should be the rule. Everyone should be learning – which means that the teacher should be learning as well. Every one should be teaching, each teaching the other. This means that learners should be allowed to share the knowledge and skills they have with each other.

Co-operatively, in collaboration with each other, in participation with each other, the group should decide what should be learned and how it is to be learned. They should decide upon acceptable levels of learning. They should decide upon some of the evaluation methods. The teacher should make his or her special contributions. However, most of the time, the teacher should be a manager of the learning process and no more.

The discussion method. Participative learning, co-operative learning and collaborative learning are all made possible through the discussion method. This means that there should be a lot of discussion in the adult learning groups. The teacher can become a good teacher by learning to be a good discussion leader.

Independence in learning! Ultimately, the whole purpose of functional literacy classes or groups is for the adult learner to become an independent learner. The adult learner should be able to read and write messages on his or her own. More important, the adult learner should become aware of all the knowledge sources in print in the community and nearby townships, and begin to use those sources.

Learning to learn. Having knowledge available in print is not the same thing as being able to learn that knowledge. Adults must learn how to learn from printed materials.

Some of these skills are routine: how to use a library catalogue; how to ask the librarian for help; how to read the table of contents; and how to read the preface or the introduction of a book in order to know what is in the book. Some other skills are not routine: how to pose a question initially; how to reframe the question as necessary; and how to define a problem. The literacy teacher can help adult learners only if he or she has mastered the skills of learning.

Being a model to the learners. Being a literacy teacher is a big responsibility. It has been said that a teacher does not merely teach subjects; the teacher 'teaches himself/herself'. In other words, learners begin to learn what the teacher does, begin to think the thought that the teacher thinks and adopt some of the values that the teacher has. That means that teachers should not only be a good teachers but also good persons and model citizens. Teachers should value women's equality, democracy, science, environment and peace. Teachers should be persons with model behaviour in class and in the community.

THE METHODOLOGY OF FUNCTIONAL LITERACY

The methodology of functional literacy has to include a mix of methodologies: the methodologies of teaching reading, writing and numeracy. It also must deal with the methodologies of teaching economic skills and the methodologies of promoting awareness.

The most important theme in the methodology of functional literacy is integration. It is said that literacy and functionality should be so taught that the learner does not even become aware of whether he or she is learning literacy or functionality at any particular time. This is easier said than done.

We will begin by looking at the methodology of each of reading, writing, numeracy, functionality and awareness.

General methods of teaching literacy

There are numerous methods of teaching literacy to adult learners. Although many new methods have come into use, old methods also remain. A discussion on methods is useful for understanding the method in use in your particular literacy project or programme.

Focus on alphabetical languages. Let us for the present focus only on alphabetical languages of the world. Most languages in the world are alphabetical languages. The Chinese language is an exception. Japanese and Korean languages are a mix of the alphabetical and the Chinese ideograms.

Types of methods of teaching languages. Different ways of organizing methods of teaching languages have been discussed. Professor William S. Gray in *The Teaching of Reading and Writing. An International Survey* (first published by UNESCO in 1956), talked of 'synthetic' and 'analytic' methods; 'alphabetic', 'phonic', 'word' and 'sentence' methods; 'global' and 'ideovisual' methods; and 'auditory', 'visual' and 'kinaesthetic' methods (Gray, 1969, p. 75).

It is not within the scope of this *Sourcebook* to fully explain all these individual methods, or to show the differences among them. Here, we will deal with only one significant methodological theme.

The methodological theme of our times. In the world of literacy practice today, the most important theme in the teaching of literacy is that of 'the units of language' used in teaching the language. In other words, the methodological discussion is focused on whether to teach literacy by using the smallest unit of language (that is, the letter or to teach literacy by using the largest unit of language (that is, the 'whole language'). Or should we use units in between the two extremes – the word method, the sentence method, or the paragraph method? In all cases, speaking proficiency in the language of literacy is assumed.

The various methods associated with the various units of language are discussed below in the following order: alphabetic method, word method, picture-letter-word (Laubach) method, sentence method, paragraph method and whole language method.

ALPHABETIC METHOD

The alphabetic method of teaching reading and writing is surely the oldest method around. The invention of alphabets made writing possible in most of the world's languages. Alphabet charts were seen as grand achievements of cultures that had invented writing or had learned from others to commit their own languages to writing, changing speech to script. These charts were seen as systematic and complete.

Somehow the idea got hold of the minds of the newly lettered élite in almost all cultures that the teaching of reading had to be based on the alphabet chart. Generation after generation of children (and adults) experienced the tedium and boredom of learning the alphabet through drills.

These letters were then combined into simple words. Unfortunately, these simple words, used in teaching to read, were not always meaningful. Since they were chosen for their convenience in teaching reading, they were often meaningless. Teaching in English typically began with 'cat, fat, rat', or something similarly nonsensical.

These words were combined into sentences. Again, these sentences were made up for their linguistic usefulness in teaching reading and they were often artificial and meaningless. For centuries, learning to read was a difficult and boring task.

While the alphabetic method is now generally rejected, it is still in use in many literacy projects, programmes and campaigns. The well-known national literacy campaign of Ethiopia, for example, used the alphabetical method of teaching literacy. Perhaps, it continues to do so.

Ironically, illiterates often expect to learn by the alphabetic method! It is the only method they have heard about. It is the method which is sanctified in story and myth. In the programme area of Literacy House, Lucknow, India in the mid-1960s, illiterates began by rejecting the idea of learning with the help of any of those new-fangled methods. They wanted to learn the old and tried – though boring – way of the alphabetic method. It took some time to convince them of the merit in using newer global methods.

WORD METHOD

During the last half century, the methodological wall of stone protecting the alphabetic method was brought down. It was discovered that human beings can recognize complete meaningful words as they can recognize full faces of friends in large crowds. It helps if the words to be learned are meaningful. Why not, then, avoid the boredom of alphabet drilling alphabets for learning the abstract shapes of letter? Why not learn to recognize meaningful words? We would, of course, go from words back to letters later.

The idea of 'meaningfulness' of words is important. What it means is that the words chosen for teaching literacy do not have to be silly though they still have to be somewhat simple. Words chosen for study and recognition do not have to be: cat, fat, rat. Words to be learned could be picked up from the realities of learners' lives – bread, cattle, debt, health and hunger, for instance.

Obviously, the meaningfulness of words is motivational for adult learners. This motivational aspect is enhanced even further by choosing words that offer opportunities for adults to reflect on their own realities and to do something about their needs and pains. We should note that it is the word method (and even more the sentence method to be discussed below) that has made the methodological approach of Paulo Freire even possible.

FROM WORDS BACK INTO LETTERS

The word method does not ignore letters. The word method uses meaningful words first and then returns to talk about what words are made of. The movement is from words to letters.

Words are made to play their role of bringing meaningfulness and motivation to the process of learning to read. Then, the words are broken into syllables or into letters, as appropriate. Learners learn to recognize these letters. Only those few letters that formed the recognized word are learned, not the complete alphabet chart. Thus, the task of learning the alphabet is divided into many convenient parts. Learning these letters as part of meaningful words is less boring.

As a few letters are learned, these are combined in many different ways to make new words. In that way, the essential and exciting process of reading begins at the very moment of recognizing just one word. The essence of the total language process become clear.

LAUBACH'S PICTURE-LETTER-WORD METHOD AND EACH-ONE-TEACH-ONE

The literacy method associated with Laubach is essentially a word method. But there are some additional features that make it a picture-letter-word method. Pictures on a chart represent in each case the shape of the letter to be learned and a word that begins with that letter.

The 'each-one-teach-one' method of delivery of literacy is also associated with Laubach. This method of delivery services has survived better than the Laubach literacy method itself. Where groups of adults cannot be organized into classes, this approach to literacy teaching is encouraged.

SENTENCE METHOD

The 'sentence method' carries the ideas of the 'word method' to the next step. The sentence, it is said, is the most natural unit of language. So why not use the sentence as the unit of language teaching?

The question arises: 'But can non-literates recognize whole sentences?' The answer is 'Yes!' Human beings can recognize whole sentences in the same way that they can recognize rows of houses in a street or absorb the whole scene on a beach.

Why not then, use whole sentences which can be much more meaningful than individual words. Once a sentence is perceived, the string of words could be separated into words. Words could be broken into syllables or letters as appropriate.

Then the essential process of language learning begins. Learners make new words and new sentences with words and sentences already learned.

Relevance to functional literacy. It is the combination of the word method and the sentence method that made this particular method of teaching functional literacy possible. Indeed, most functional literacy primers use the sentence method. The first sentence in one of the primers written for learners in the United Republic of Tanzania, for example, was:

Pamba ni Mali. [Cotton is Wealth.]

The sentence was broken into three words – *Pamba, ni* and *Mali.* Then the words were broken into syllables – Pa, mba, ni, ma, li. Syllables were broken into letters *a, b, i, l, m, n, p.*

Kiswahili is a syllabic language. The syllables learned were therefore used later to make new words – *mama* (mother), *lima* (cultivate), *mamba* (cobra), and so forth.

Relevance to emancipatory literacy. As we have indicated earlier, the combination of the word method and the sentence method also made the emancipatory method of literacy possible. Paulo Freire's 'literacy for liberation' and his 'pedagogy of the oppressed' would not perhaps have been possible using the alphabetic method of teaching literacy, because Freire would not have been able to begin teaching with words and sentences loaded with themes of liberation. Without the sentence method, illiterate adults would not have been able to read their world in words and sentences such as these – Why are we hungry? Why are our children dying?

Paragraph method

The paragraph method is another step beyond the sentence method. The assumption is that meanings do not reside in single sentences. Units of thought take a two to three sentence paragraph to complete the thought. In the paragraph method whole paragraphs are handled as units of language.

Whole language method

It is a big leap from the paragraph method to the 'whole language method'. With hindsight, it seems the most natural thing to happen! The seeds of the whole language approach were sown in the writing of Dewey, the famous American philosopher of education. Its time has come now, in a big way!

What is whole language method? Anna Cresswell of Canada answers thus: 'It is not a programme, it is not a big book, it is not how you rearrange the desks in your classroom... It is a mindset, an attitude...it is truly integrated language arts'. In other words, whole language approach is a way of viewing language as whole – speaking, listening, reading and writing.

Cresswell lists other key elements as: 'the creation of a language-rich, success-oriented, noncompetitive environment; students making choices about their learning; a variety of materials; an emphasis on process and attitude rather than on product; and a less formal evaluation process'. Andrea Butler of Australia adds: 'Keeping language "whole" requires classrooms that maintain the social, functional and aesthetic aspects of language'. Clearly evaluation in the whole language approach has to be learner-centred.

The whole language approach is eminently suitable for functional literacy. It provides the mindset and is the most congenial to group discussion. The combination of word method and the sentence method provide the concrete steps of teaching reading.

TEACHING READING IN NON-ALPHABETICAL LANGUAGES

The discussion above applies only to developments in the methodology of teaching literacy in the alphabetical languages. These remarks do not apply fully to the methodology of teaching languages in which writing is based on characters.

It should be noted, however, that characters of the Chinese language, for example, are also undergoing abstraction. In other words, a standard set of strokes is being developed and used to develop new characters and relevant meanings from old characters.

Since to read and write the Chinese language one has to learn to recognize characters, it comes very close to learning sight words in the alphabetical languages. These characters cannot be broken down into parts in the same way in which words in the alphabetical languages can be broken down. Methodologies of teaching languages using the sentence method, the paragraph method and the whole language approach will perhaps be somewhat applicable to teaching literacy in logographic languages as well.

General methods of teaching writing

Writing is not the same cognitive skill as reading. Writing is a deeper, more challenging skill. No wonder most of us learn to read earlier than we learn to write. Some learners read quite well, even though they are unable to write. We are, of course, making a distinction between writing and copying – mere copying is possible without the ability to read in a language.

USE OF WRITING IN THE TEACHING OF READING

Most literacy programmes prefer to teach reading and writing together. The belief is that reading and writing together make a mind meeting – the bond between reading and writing should never be broken.

Indeed, writing is often used to reinforce reading. First, letters or words may be copied. Then they may be reconstructed from memory. Writing of letters and words from memory means mastery of the material read.

TEACHING OF WRITING

Although it is not taken seriously, there is some discussion about the advisability of not teaching writing during the first stages of teaching literacy. It is suggested that the teaching of writing takes too much time and the teaching of reading should therefore get preference over the teaching of writing. Others argue for the necessity to teach reading and writing together but are not clear about how to combine the two to get the best results.

FROM PENMANSHIP TO CLAIMING A VOICE

Our conception of writing has exploded and with it the methods of teaching writing. Writing is not merely penmanship, but to claim a voice. Thus, on the one hand, learning to write means learning to write legibly. On the other hand, it means learning to reflect on one's reality, to learn to represent it in writing, and to have the courage and conviction to share it with others.

Teaching and learning penmanship. To teach writing as penmanship, a variety of time-tested techniques are available. For example, writing letters and words in large sizes on large surfaces helps in learning to make good curves and loops. If chalk and chalkboard are not available, then a stick used on sand or clay is all right.

When teaching to write on paper, penmanship lessons begin with learning how to hold a pen or pencil. Workbooks especially printed to teach good writing habits may be available in some literacy programmes. If they are not, the teacher should demonstrate good writing both in the group and in individual settings. After that practice should make perfect! (see Figures 5.1 and 5.2).

SOME SUGGESTED EXERCISES

Sohan Singh (1976) suggested six steps in learning writing: (i) copying words written by the teacher on the blackboard; (ii) copying words or letters in the workbook; (iii) writing words dictated by the teacher; (iv) correcting mis-spelt words; (v) filling in blanks by writing single words

Exercise in building up and taking apart words

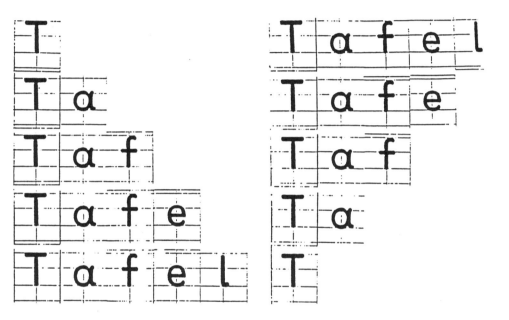

The exercise starts either with the whole word or with the first letter of a word. Going across the page, one letter after another is either added or taken away. *Every* stage is read out loud. Since each stage usually makes no sense on its own, the reader must rely entirely on the individual letters. This exercise is also sometimes useful for more advanced readers who often try to help themselves by guessing, but who are not able to read a strange word letter by letter when they make a wrong guess.

Figure 5.1 Helping adult learners learn how to write (from Writing Workshop for New Readers and Writers in Bremen, 1988)

Figure 5.2 Helping adult learners how to write (from a text in German, Klett, Stuttgart, 1989)

in sentences as part of exercises in the workbook; and (vi) writing words and sentences of significance to the participants.

Writing with a purpose. At a later stage in literacy learning, the emphasis could change. Writing in the lives of most people plays a functional role – writing messages, writing notes to help remember, making lists of addresses, keeping accounts, etc. A few people will also write to codify significant knowledge. A few more will write for expressive and creative purposes.

It follows that at the functional level, the teaching of writing should include the teaching of keeping accounts, recording dates of births of children, writing diaries and journals, etc. Other expository exercises such as writing letters, applications, appeals and so on should also be provided.

Writing as expression: claiming a voice. The teaching of writing as expression is getting more and more attention today. There is a move towards the democratization of creativity, towards helping people to claim a voice.

In developing expressive writing skills one should be taught to begin with personal narratives. Then, one should tap into other life experiences. The use of writing dialogue has been recommended by some writing specialists as a way of acquiring facility in writing. Stories, myths and oral history are good subject matter for a beginning creative writer.

Combining writing with publishing. Some teachers of writing suggest that writing should be connected with publishing. Adults' writing should be published in book form for use by the group, but preferably for use in the community.

The International Reading Association (United States) has different interest groups working under it. One such interest groups is concerned with adult literacy. In the Spring 1991 issue of their newsletter, they published a short article by Barbara Bergin, 'Why Publish?' She talks of two literacy programmes – one in Kentucky and another in Vermont – that have published materials written by adult learners to be read by other adult learners.

She tells us this material is thought-provoking, relevant and from real-life. The experiences described range from a hunting accident to child abuse to left-handedness. These publications have appeared both in book form and as monthly newspapers.

Barbara Bergin has summarized the benefits of publishing writings of adults learners as follows:

Benefits to learners:

- increased sense of pride in self and self-esteem

- a good sense of personal recognition

- a sense of identification with other learners, seen and unseen

- lessened feelings of personal inadequacy or isolation

- greater motivation to read and write

- increased communication among learners

- meaningful collaboration among learners and teachers.

Benefits to programmes:

- a way of increasing learner motivations

- improved attendance in groups and fewer dropouts

- increased public awareness of and interest in the programme – public relations tool for recruitment and for fund raising

- demonstration of the programme's effectiveness

- publication of relevant reading materials

- a way of implementing the whole language approach to the teaching of literacy

- linkages with the community and the workplace.

TEACHERS AS EXAMPLES

Adult learners will not have the courage to write unless teachers become an example to them. Teachers should write as well. They should write logs and journals. They should keep anecdotal records. Most of all they should share their writings with adult learners. The classroom newspaper is a first-rate joint project for literacy teachers and literacy learners.

General methods of teaching numeracy

Too often, numeracy – like literacy – is a silent partner in functional literacy programmes. Some of the most important works on literacy ignore numeracy.

We know that numeracy is a cognitive process separate from the teaching of reading and writing. Illiterate individuals may be numerate. Many from trading families in Punjab, India, though illiterate may be amazingly numerate. They can work with multiple numbers and various operations, all in their heads while they may not be able to put anything on paper or read anything. They learn their arithmetic through drill and memorization in an oral institution called the Pandha.

There is also a difference between the ability to understand text containing quantitative information and the ability to perform mathematical operations used to generate the quantitative information presented in the text.

_____

METHODS OF TEACHING NUMERACY IN FUNCTIONAL LITERACY

There is agreement that basic numeracy should be required for functional literacy. There is no agreement, however, on what basic numeracy skills should be taught and how.

A common sense approach suggests that basic arithmetical operations should be taught as well as everyday applications. Addition and subtraction, comparison in length, weight and volume, dates and time must be included. In today's world, adults should be able to read their watches, both the old watches and new digital watches. They should, of course, understand the difference between digital representations and decimals.

_____

METHODS OF TEACHING NUMERACY

By way of the methods of teaching numeracy to adults within the context of functional literacy, the following general principles should be mentioned.

1. Adults must be made aware that they have already acquired quite a bit of oral numeracy and that, in most cases, it will not be a question of learning to count, add and subtract; it will be a matter of learning to do it on paper.

2. Not only should adults be assured of the numeracy they already have, but they should also be helped to acquire some excitement about the magic of numbers. There is too much mystification about arithmetic in school and out of school. Arithmetic should be demystified.

_____

FIRST THE NUMBERS

In teaching of numeracy, the numbers 0, 1, 2, 3, 4, 5, 6, 7, 8 and 9 must be properly learned. This learning will have to involve recognition and writing drills.

_____

THEN, THE PLACE VALUES

This is where the magic of arithmetic should begin. The concept of place values should be taught. Adults should understand how with nine numbers and a zero, the smallest and the largest numbers possible in the world can be written down by assigning proper place values.

Adult learners should then be helped to understand the necessity of writing numbers in perfectly straight rows and columns. They should also understand the need to write each numeral exactly in the row and column to which it should belong in a particular setting.

THE FOUR BASIC OPERATIONS

Arithmetic is a subject with completely systematic structure. Every numeracy primer will be found to follow more or less the same logic and sequence.

In teaching the four basic operations (addition, subtraction, multiplication and division), the literacy teacher should follow the numeracy primer or the lessons on numeracy in the general literacy primer.

The only thing the teacher can do is to point out the connections between these abstract exercises and the real-life needs. The teacher should have adult learners find specific instances in daily life that require numeracy and then have them invent solutions to share.

COMMON FRACTIONS, DECIMALS AND PERCENTAGES

It will depend upon the curriculum established within a particular project, programme or campaign, but it is necessary for adult learners at some stage to become familiar with the various types of fractions.

Once again, the literacy teacher should follow the numeracy primer being used within his or her programme. A general suggestion can be made. The teacher should show connections between fractions, decimals and percentages and the day-to-day life of the farmers and workers. These day-to-day practices in the lives of farmers and workers will include measuring lengths and volumes, comparing prices, making solutions for pesticide control, borrowing at the credit union, or otherwise walking through today's literate environment.

STARTING FROM THE OTHER END: POINTING OUT ARITHMETICAL NEEDS OF REAL LIFE

Finally, the literacy teacher should start from the other end: that is, from the day-to-day lives of adult learners. The arithmetical needs of their daily lives should be listed and expressed as problems of arithmetic. This is also the time to help people understand digital watches, simple line graphs and pie-charts that appear in newspapers and government publications.

Games and simulations. The teaching of arithmetic can be made interesting for learners. Learners can be invited to design games and simulations wherein newly-learned arithmetical skills can be practised. The arithmetical needs of traditional games can be brought out. New games can be developed for enjoyable practice of arithmetical skills.

Methods of integrating the 3 R's into the teaching of functional literacy

An important methodological theme in functional literacy is integration. First, there should be complete integration among the 3 R's – reading, writing and arithmetic. Then the integration of the 3 R's should be expanded to include functionality. Of course, awareness should also become integrated into the total curriculum.

However, even the integration of the 3 R's itself has often been less than perfect. Teaching reading and writing together in early stages has been possible. Writing has been used to reinforce recognition of letters, words and short sentences. However, in later stages, integration has not worked easily. Writing has taken a back seat.

Integrating numeracy with the teaching of reading and writing has been even more difficult. The only integration possible has been by way of an add-on. Typically, numbers have been added at the end of each reading lesson in the primer. Later, a separate numeracy book may be provided, if at all.

Integrating the teaching of functional skills with the teaching of literacy

The concept of integration of literacy and functionality are at the core of a definition of functional literacy.

INTEGRATION WITHIN LIMITS

As we have discussed elsewhere, the development of the word method, the sentence method and the whole language method made the integration between functionality and literacy possible – but within limits.

Limited integration is possible because under the new methods, the very first words or sentences of the primer can include some very very simple functional content, for example 'cotton is wealth', 'man is health', 'to plan is to choose', and so forth.

Integration remains limited, however, because after the initial phase of language learning, the logic of learning the language and the logic in the hierarchy of functional content to be learned are not parallel and are quite difficult to integrate. Integration is not only inherently difficult, it

पाठ एक   पाठ 1

एकता एक ताकत

पढ़िए :

| ए | क | एक
| त | तक
| T | काका ताका एका काता

Figure 5.3 First lesson from a literacy primer for adults in Hindi. It deals with a topic of awareness - the need for communal solidarity among various religious groups in India. The teaching method could be described as the picture-word association method. The words are broken down in alphabets. Alphabets are combined into new words. (Literacy Kit issued by the Directorate of Adult Education, New Delhi.)

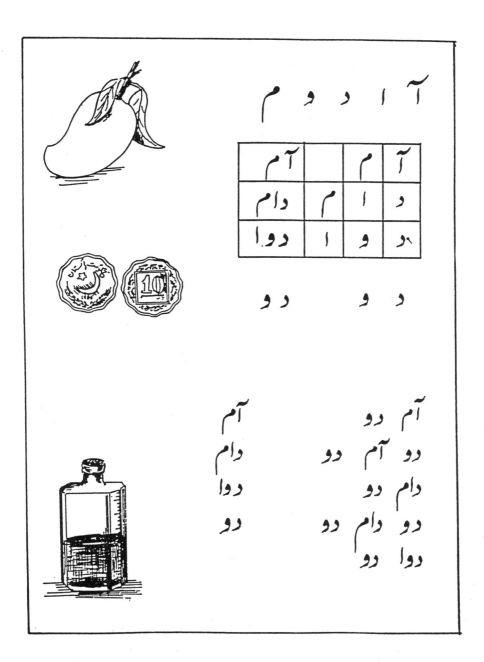

Figure 5.4 First page from a primer in Urdu. Picture and word association are used to learn components of words. The picture is used to evoke the learning of alphabets later used in the associated word. New words are made by combining alphabets. The content deals with a fruit, coins and medicine. (From Allama Iqbal Open University, 1987.)

is also impractical in terms of the resources required for producing thematic units to fit multiple needs. Integration also requires a better-trained teaching force.

THE FUNCTIONAL LITERACY METHOD AS INTEGRATOR

The method of teaching functional literacy at the initial stage has become more or less standard:

- A typical lesson begins with an illustration and an associated sentence. This sentence is as short as possible.

- The sentence has some very simple functional content. Often this content is attitudinal.

- The sentence is read and re-read to establish a level of recognition of the sentence and its parts.

- The sentence is then broken into its component words.

- Then time is spent to establish recognition of words until they become sight words.

- Words are then broken into syllables and letters, as appropriate.

- Time is spent to establish recognition of syllables and letters.

- Then the reverse process starts. Letters and/or syllables are used to make new syllables or words as appropriate.

- Words are used to make new sentences.

This is how literacy is learned. See the two illustrations of the first pages of two literacy primers, one in Hindi, the other in Urdu (Figures 5.3 and 5.4).

METHODS OF TEACHING FUNCTIONALITY

There are limits to the degree of functional knowledge that can be integrated with literacy. It must be taught as a separate but parallel stream. But what are the methods of teaching functional knowledge?

The only useful statement that can be made in this regard is this: the methodology of teaching functionality will have to be a mix of the methodology of agricultural extension and the methodology of vocational education. It will involve discussion, demonstration, guided practice on the experimental farm or in the factory shed and field work.

INCOME-GENERATING ENTERPRISES

The natural culmination of functionality within the context of functional literacy programmes is an income-generating enterprise which a learner group develops and establishes for generating income for themselves or the community. Whatever else such enterprises may involve, they do require good management.

It is not within the scope of this *Sourcebook* to deal with methods of agricultural extension and vocational education in general. Nor can we deal with methods of discussion, demonstration, guided practice and field activities. Similarly, management of enterprises is a subject matter in its own right and has its own methodological content.

Organizers of literacy programmes must be aware of the need of this content and of the need for suitable methods for teaching various parts of this content.

FUNCTIONALITY: ULTIMATELY, A MATTER OF KNOWLEDGE

As said elsewhere, you do not just read, you always read something. That something carries knowledge. Unfortunately, this knowledge can be superficial or meaningless. Some knowledge can be mis-knowledge that misleads.

Functional literacy that includes literacy, functionality and awareness will seek to communicate considerable knowledge to adult readers. That is good. But that does not mean that this knowledge should not be examined critically. Just because something has been printed in the primer or in a book does not make it God's truth.

Knowledge included in primers, in graded books and in discussion guides can be specific. We have to learn to generalize it. We have to learn to transfer it to other situations. What is learned on one machine should be made usable on almost all machines in that family of machines. What is learned about pest control in a cotton field should be generalizable to all pest control. What is learned about human health should illuminate problems of the health of the cattle.

Again, knowledge included in primers, and in graded books and other related materials can be scattered in pieces. It must be organized into what Thomas Sticht calls 'coherent bodies of knowledge'. Coherent bodies of knowledge are easier to expand and to build upon.

Promoting awareness

The word 'conscientization' was given to literacy workers by Paulo Freire in the beginning of the 1970s. The word meant raising the consciousness of common people about the world in which they lived. The message was that the conditions of poverty and exploitation were not God-given. The poor and the oppressed were told that they should understand the relationships in which they are caught. They were told that the economic relations, social relations and political relations in which they were imprisoned should be understood and then changed.

Later on the words 'critical consciousness' and 'awareness' came to be used in place of conscientization. Today, perhaps, 'awareness' is the most popular choice.

AWARENESS OF WHAT?

As we discussed earlier, awareness used to be a radical idea. The awareness was about relationships. It was about economic relationships – why are some so poor and some so rich? It was about social relationships – why some have so much status and prestige and others do not. It was about political relationships – why are some people so powerful and all others so powerless? It was about cultural relationships – why the culture of the poor is held in low esteem and ridiculed.

In many projects and programmes, it so happens that the word 'awareness' is diluted. Awareness may mean no more than an awareness of the government programmes and how the poor can avail themselves of those programmes.

In the preceding chapter, we pointed out that the concept of awareness has come to acquire many different meanings. Of course, there will be many different methods to communicate all those different meanings.

THE ESSENTIAL METHOD OF CREATING AWARENESS

The methodology of promoting awareness has to be moral and dialogic at the same time. It has to be moral because people have to be helped to become aware about existing realities and to want to transform them – in the context of a set of preferred values.

The methodology also has to be dialogic, that is, it has to be genuinely educational. Those engaged in the process of promoting awareness have to be real adult educators. They are not in the business of shaping individual behaviour or manipulating groups.

BRINGING IT ALL TOGETHER: DISCUSSIONS OF THEMES FOR ACTION

Ultimately all of this must be brought together – reading, writing, numeracy, functional skills and awareness. How do we do all this?

At one level, integration will be achieved because all content (literacy, functionality and awareness) will be taught to the same group of learners. At another level, the co-ordination of content will be brought about by thematic integration. Different themes will be chosen which will appear in all aspects of the learning experience – literacy, functionality and awareness.

THINGS TO DO OR THINK ABOUT

1. What is the 'methodology' of literacy being used in your literacy project, programme or campaign?

2. Are you as a teacher able to see the methodology of teaching reading actually at work within the primer and other teaching materials? What is the methodology?

3. Are you clear about how integration among various components of your literacy programme – literacy, functional knowledge and awareness – is achieved?

4. Are you satisfied with the integration you are able to achieve personally within your literacy class? What theme or themes have you found so far to be the best for combining all interests?

5. What are some of the interesting methods you have used in the teaching of reading, writing, numeracy, functionality and awareness?

Chapter Six

Functional Literacy Materials for Teachers and Learners

What materials are needed for teaching functional literacy? What materials are needed by learners? What materials are needed by teachers? What is special about functional literacy materials? How are different teaching materials brought together? These are the questions addressed in this chapter.

Literacy teachers have to be interested in the questions above. The reason is obvious. If methodology is the soul of functional literacy, then materials are the body of the functional literacy programmes. In a sense, doing literacy work is using functional literacy materials with adult groups.

Teaching–learning materials are not independent of other decisions. Your definition of literacy (Chapters 1 and 2) will directly influence your materials. The same is true about your clients and your curriculum. These too will influence your materials. Finally, the specific content of functionality and awareness (Chapters 3 and 4) and your methodologies for teaching and integrating this content (Chapter 5) will determine what materials are designed and produced.

The contents of this chapter are treated under eight headings.

- What is special about functional literacy materials?
- A typical package of functional literacy materials
- Using functional literacy materials to best advantage
- Focus on the primer: the method within the lesson
- Materials for teaching functional skills
- Materials for promoting awareness
- How to train teachers to use functional literacy materials
- Teacher- and learner-made materials.

WORDS OF WISDOM AND VOICES FROM THE REAL WORLD

> If you want to bring about significant change in an educational pro-
> gramme or system, simply change the materials with which teachers
> and learners work. (Professor Edgar Dale *in his seminar at Ohio State
> University*)

Teaching materials express our philosophies and our methodologies.
Surely the most concrete and the most visible aspect of a literacy programme is the package of teaching–learning materials used. It is in the
teaching–learning materials that our philosophies of development and
education find expression, that our teaching methodologies become
concrete. The package of teaching–learning materials reveals a lot about
a literacy programme. Teaching–learning materials used in a functional
literacy project or programme are special in terms of their content, their
methodological design and their variety.

The obvious necessity to know functional literacy materials. Those working
in a functional literacy programme must be fully familiar with their
materials. They must know both the total package of functional literacy
materials and each individual item in the total set of materials – the
primer, the wall charts, the graded books and the teacher's guide. They
must know the message and the method built into each instructional item
in the package.

Literacy teachers at the grassroots must be familiar with the materials
designed and published by the project or programme. Only then will
they be able to adapt them to local needs and to produce some materials
locally, to meet specific local needs.

Perspective on locally-produced materials. Some functional literacy programmes have required that most if not all of the instructional materials
be prepared in the field. This is possible in pilot projects that are at the
same time engaged in action research. However, this is an unreasonable
expectation of typical community-based literacy workers. Therefore, our
expectation of workers at the grassroots is more modest. We expect them
to understand their materials well so that they can adapt them or add to
them some locally-made materials to meet specific local needs.

In this chapter, we seek to help literacy teachers and other grassroots
workers understand the types and uses of functional literacy materials.
This general discussion will help them understand their own materials
now in use in their programmes. We hope that this discussion will help
them use their materials more effectively and to adapt them to local

needs, and guide them in preparing locally-relevant materials. Finally, it may help them contribute to the revision of their materials when revised editions are planned to be published.

What is special about functional literacy materials?

There are two things which are special about teaching–learning materials in a functional literacy project, programme or campaign: a direct and clear interest in teaching some economic skills that increase the productivity of farmers and workers, or generate secondary income for their families; and an attempt to integrate the teaching of literacy skills and economic skills.

Some topics of health and hygiene are also added. When the promotion of awareness is an honest additional goal, the teaching of awareness is also integrated into the teaching of the other two components.

Even a quick look at a package of functional literacy materials indicates an 'economic' interest written into the content of the teaching and learning materials. We should remember our earlier discussion concerning the 'advantages of economic motivations' for literacy in poor countries of the Third World. That will help us understand why there is so much focus on teaching economically functional skills.

Those who favour the economic bias in functional literacy materials tell us that there is no harm in emphasizing economic motivations. This approach motivates learners but need not imprison them in the mere bread-and-butter facts of life. Indeed, learners quickly generalize their motivations from economic to other non-material motivations and greatly expand their horizons.

The awareness component of functional literacy is harder to include in teaching–learning materials. Materials related to awareness can not avoid political issues and hence literacy programmes avoid such materials. While issues of freedom and justice are timeless, concrete questions of freedom and justice change day by day. Providing useful teaching–learning materials dealing with the awareness component of functional literacy is thus difficult. Furthermore, leading a useful discussion on issues of awareness is most challenging and not all grassroots workers are able to handle such discussions. As a result, the awareness component of functional literacy is neglected in functional literacy materials. Some of the so-called awareness materials may be no more than government propaganda for plans and information on some local schemes of development.

We have talked of functional materials separately from awareness materials because these are often designed and produced as separate items in the instructional materials kit. In reality, economics cannot be separated from politics and functional materials are therefore also political. Functional materials, for example, may simply train for higher productivity or may seek to promote some sort of economic democracy. Literacy teachers should be aware of this reality and should share this understanding with their learners.

A typical package of functional literacy materials

To teach functional literacy effectively, one must teach literacy, functionality and awareness. It is obvious that materials are needed to teach all of those components.

The nature of objectives in each of the three components are quite different. Hence there is a need a variety of functional literacy materials.

Table 6.1 Three components of functional literacy programmes and their teaching/learning materials

	Teaching–learning materials
Literacy	Print materials of all kinds.
Functionality	Materials for teaching and demonstrating economic skills. That would mean access to demonstration plots, tools andequipment, and printed materials for support of literacy and functionality.
Awareness	A different set of teaching strategies and a different set of materials. There may be printed materials, discussion sheets, socio-dramas, puppet plays, popular theatre and use of the media (radio, television and newspaper).

The teaching–learning kit of functional literacy materials includes a variety of items. To understand their nature and functions, these items can be organized into types and categories in several different ways. The ideal materials needed are typically never available.

It has been suggested that it is sensible to think of post-literacy activities before planning and implementing a literacy programme. Others have talked of the need of a well-planned pre-literacy stage. It should be useful to think of material preparation in terms of the following grid depicted in Table 6.2.

Table 6.2 Materials for pre-literacy, literacy and post-literacy activities

	Teaching–learning materials
Pre-literacy	Messages in the environment: on bags of flour and sugar; on tea bags and cups; on buses and bus stands; on toilets; on bill boards; on bills and receipts.
Literacy	Primers and wall charts; materials to teach numeracy and literacy; and graded books.
Post-literacy	Follow-up books; magazines; trade books and media clubs.

The examples in Table 6.2 are not complete. One can think of other examples of materials for each of the three types of literacy. Once again, what is ideally possible is not typically available within real projects and programmes.

Materials of functional literacy could also be organized in terms of media as shown in Table 6.3.

Table 6.3 Media used in functional literacy activities

	Teaching–learning materials
Folk media	Songs, recitations, folk stories, oral history, drums, dances; popular theatre, puppet plays and other art.
Print media	Primers, wall charts, flash cards, flannel graphs, leaflets, folders and booklets.
Electronic media	Tape recorder, radio, television, VCR and computers.

Of course, what materials actually constitute the package of functional literacy materials depends on the culture and technology of a setting. Computers may be in use in the United States of America, but not in Bolivia. Folk media may be in use in India and Papua New Guinea, not so much in Saudi Arabia.

Yet, another way of organizing the materials and media of functional literacy is in terms of control of media (see Table 6.4).

Table 6.4 Media control for functional learning activities

Teaching–learning materials	
Local control	Materials made by teachers and learners.
Programme control	Primers, follow-up books, andeverything else designed and centrally-produced by the project.
State/corporate control	Newspapers, trade books, radio and television

Finally, and most important, the materials may be divided in terms of the predominant user (see Table 6.5).

Once again, the variety of materials and their technology depends on the culture and technology of the setting in which the materials are put to use.

THE NECESSITY FOR GOOD TEACHERS' MATERIALS

It seems obvious that projects and programmes should not cut corners on the teachers guides. These guides should supply both the methodology of teaching and substantive knowledge. If the teacher is unable to handle economic skills, nothing much can be taught to learners. If the teacher lacks awareness, promotion of awareness among learners is unlikely. To put literacy to work for development, the teacher must be knowledgeable enough to be an agent of change.

Using functional literacy materials to best advantage

An entire book can be written on the use of functional literacy materials and media. In the brief space of this section, we present the most important ideas.

Table 6.5 Teachers' and learners' materials for functional literacy activities

Materials for teachers	Materials for learners
Print	
Teacher's guide for literacy teaching	Primer
Wall charts connected with the primer (or the chalkboard)	Writing exercise books
	Numeracy exercise books
Flashcards	
Flannelgraphs	
Teacher's guide for conducting discussions of local significance in a 'Study Circle' context	Discussion sheets
	Leaflets
Teacher's handbook on skill demonstrations	Demonstration sheets
Instructions on testing	Testing materials
Teacher's materials	Follow-up books
Teacher's materials	Radio
Teacher's materials	Television/VCR
Teacher's materials	Computer and software

Some essential ideas must be kept in mind about the use of functional literacy materials. First, the literacy teacher must become fully familiar with the materials before bringing them to the class or the group for use. The supervisor should be consulted if there is any confusion or misunderstanding. Second, the literacy teacher should be able to look at the total set of materials as a system, understanding the contribution each item makes to the total instruction, and the combinations and general sequence in which various items will be used. Third, the literacy teacher should be able to make effective and efficient use of each of the items of teaching–learning materials in the total set, package or system (see Figure 6.1).

A few suggestions about the uses of a variety of functional literacy materials are given below.

The chalkboard. Almost every literacy teacher will use some sort of chalkboard. Typical errors made in the use of the chalkboard are the following:

- The chalkboard is not kept clean enough.
- The chalkboard has lost all its paint and needs to be repainted.
- The chalkboard is hung on a tree so that is not directly visible to all learners and it keeps swaying in the wind.
- The literacy teacher stands in front of the chalkboard blocking his or her own work on the board.

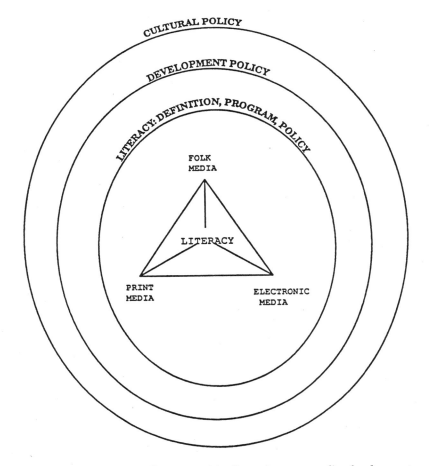

Figure 6.1 The linkages among literacy and media and among media, development and culture
Computer graphic by Kenichi Kubota, 1991

- The teacher writes very small letters or numbers so that learners can not read them.

- The teacher does not write legibly, does not write in straight lines or does not make good use of chalkboard space.

The literacy primer. We will discuss the method of the primer and the structure of the lessons in functional literacy primers later. Here we point out only that the teacher should ensure that every class member has been taught to care for his or her primer. Learners must not tear up the pages of the primer or spoil it with food and water.

Once learners are in the group, the teacher should make sure that everyone has access to the primer, and that everyone has found the page and line which will be studied that day.

The wall charts. The comments concerning chalkboards also apply to wall charts. These should be displayed so that they are not fluttering in the wind and are visible to everyone. The teacher should not stand in front of them while teaching.

How to use an invited guest. It is important to prepare well for an invited guest. Explain to the future guest your expectations of him or her. Ask the future guest about how you should prepare yourself and the group beforehand. Receive the guest at a place agreed upon before and accompany him or her to the group. Guests can get lost if they are not received at a proper place! Take due time to introduce the invited guest. You must leave time for questions from the group. At the end summarize the main points of the guest's remarks and those raised in the discussion.

Demonstrations. Too many demonstrations fail to teach because the demonstrator is not visible to all learners. The demonstrator does not explain what is being done and why. The do's and don't's of completing the task being demonstrated should be clearly explained. Since the demonstrator is typically facing the adult learners, the demonstrator's right hand is the learner's left hand, and the demonstrator's left hand is the learner's right hand. This can sometimes create serious problems and should be properly explained. Demonstrations should always be followed by practice by learners themselves.

Local study groups and action groups as learning strategies. As the name suggest, local study groups and action groups are community-level groups. They come into being around some community problems. They undertake to study a problem, and organize themselves and the community to take actions to solve the problem. The literacy teacher can encourage adults in literacy groups to come together in study and action groups to solve community problems raised inside the literacy group or outside in the community.

If the members of the study and action group are not yet proficient in literacy, a literate member can be recruited from the community to bring to the group information that is available only in print.

Teachers do not have to attend all meetings of a particular group, but they must do all they can do to bring these groups into being.

A puppet show, a popular theatre, a radio programme, a television programme, or a film show. In each case, the literacy teacher should prepare the adult group to receive instruction through these media. After the group has listened to the radio broadcast or seen the puppet, film or television show, there should be a discussion focusing on what was learned.

Sports, games and physical culture. All cultures play. In fact some philosophers have described cultures as games. Important educational uses can be made of sports, games and physical culture. Literacy and numeracy can be put to use in keeping scores, writing items for the rural newspaper, and writing descriptions and rules of traditional games to save them for the coming generations.

A follow-up book. All of the things discussed above – and follow-up books in particular – can be used within the context of a study group or circle. A study group is a group of people who volunteer to come together as a group, at regular intervals of time, to discuss a topic about which they have first learned by reading, listening or viewing. Chapter 7 looks in greater detail at how study groups are effectively developed and led by teachers and learners.

Focus on the primer: the method within the lesson

In some functional literacy projects, learners are given loose lesson sheets from which to learn. These sheets are given, one at a time, at suitable intervals. Complete and bound primers are not used.

The assumption is that complete and bound primers are seen by the illiterate as too big and difficult. They are afraid that the illiterate will decide to escape the impossible task by dropping out. On the other hand, the single lesson sheet will be seen as being manageable. The learner will get the next sheet when he or she is ready to tackle it.

Not all literacy workers agree with the above assumptions. In any case, the advantages of lesson sheets are few and the disadvantages are many. We favour the use of the complete and bound primer.

THE METHOD WITHIN THE FUNCTIONAL LITERACY PRIMER AND THE STRUCTURE OF EACH LESSON

As we have mentioned several times, the method of functional literacy is (i) the use of the 'sentence method' in teaching literacy and (ii) the 'integration' of the teaching of literacy and the teaching of functional content.

There may be some repetition of earlier content in order to ensure that this section is complete in itself.

The structure of each lesson follows a standard format that goes like this:

A sentence with functional content is presented, for instance: *Pamba ni mali.* [Cotton is wealth in Kiswahili.]

The sentence is broken into words.

Pamba ni mali

The words are broken down into syllables.

Pa mba ni mali

The syllables are broken down into letters.

p a m b a n i m a l i

In subsequent lessons, when learners seem ready, they are taught the opposite process of making syllables from letters, words from letters and sentences from words:

ma + mba = mamba (cobra)

li + ma = lima (to cultivate)

Since learners deal with meaningful words and sentences, and since these words and sentences often have functional content, they are motivated to persist in learning the process of reading and writing.

Materials for teaching functional skills

A useful distinction has been made between learning functional knowledge and learning functional skills, and then between learning skills and developing income-generating activities.

Teaching–learning functional 'knowledge'. Teaching this component of functionality is no different from teaching any content area.

Teaching–learning functional 'skills'. We have already made several references to the kinds of materials needed for teaching functional skills. Of course, the economic skill being taught will determine content and, therefore, the method.

Generally speaking, the kinds of materials used are actual tools or implements or models of such tools and implements, and demonstrations in the field or in the factory under conditions similar to the real-world settings.

One must remember, however, that charts, posters and other display materials can and indeed should be used to support use of tools in demonstrations. Suitable print materials to support demonstration and practice should also be used. It is important that the 'literacy' component of practical skills is clearly brought out and taught.

Income-generating activities.These require a more expanded set of skills including entrepreneurship, management, marketing, accounting and public relations for continued market development.

Everywhere in the Third World where income-generating activities are taught, learners have asked that such skills be taught to them. Materials will, of course, vary in regard to content, needs and contexts.

Materials for promoting awareness

We have discussed the concept of awareness at several places in the *Sourcebook*. We have pointed out that the content of awareness varies in interesting ways from one literacy programme to another. Here we take up one most significant definition – awareness as empowerment.

The objectives of promoting awareness are to empower people both psychologically, as individuals, and collectively, as groups and communities. The objectives are to teach them their rights and duties, and to enable them to exercise choices.

Psychological empowerment. Psychological empowerment can be promoted by helping people understand their social, economic and political relations. To this understanding must be added feeling – a sense of scandal about existing realities. The learners should also accept the idea that they can do something about it.

Some of this sense of empowerment is inherent in literacy. Once people learn to read, they acquire a sense of independence and control over their lives. But it is necessary to promote psychological empowerment in its own right as well.

Collective or structural empowerment. Collective or structural empower-ment is more than psychological feeling. People feel empowered when they organize and then solve local problems.

For structural empowerment there has to be understanding of how structures work. Who has power? How did the powerful acquire power? What do they do with this power? Built on this understanding there should be action. This is what Paulo Freire called praxis.

In more mundane terms, we could say that active study and action groups should come into being for the structural empowerment of people in communities.

To join feeling with understanding, materials and methods of teaching awareness should be able to bring the unknown world into the learners' lives – through films and television – and to help the learners lay bare the injustices and indignities of existing relationships and to experience new relationships – through psycho-drama and socio-drama, scenarios, simulations, rural theatre and folk media.

Reading materials are necessary for providing the foundation for understanding of structures.

How to train teachers to use functional literacy materials

Economizing on the training of teachers is a false economy. Literacy teachers must be given adequate training.

Teacher training must pay sufficient attention to materials of func-tional literacy. Indeed, a large part of training should be spent on learning about the use of materials.

While mechanical patterns and routines of use of various materials have to be learned, teachers must be given enough information on why they are asked to do certain things. Otherwise even the simplest tasks can be mishandled. Remember the story of a literacy teacher in the United Republic of Tanzania who started a drill in class and could not stop! He did not know the reasons for drills and had not been taught to read the cues in the class to be able to stop at the right time!

INTEGRATING ALL MATERIALS

Teachers should be enabled to see the hidden connection between and among all media and materials. Figure 6.1 should be examined again. It helps us realize that, indeed, during our lifetime, literacy has come to be the vital centre of all media.

Print media, of course, cannot be used without literacy, either by the teacher or by the learner. Electronic media have not been able to bypass literacy as it was hoped at one time. Radio and television have not made literacy redundant. Indeed, the print media and electronic media are in a long embrace. Without literacy, the users of radio and television get less out of these media. With literacy, the media are better understood.

Finally, folk media personnel are developing new relationships with literacy. Folk songs and stories are now being put into print to enrich existing cultures.

Teacher- and learner-made materials

Community and locality are sacred words in adult literacy and adult education. We should serve community interests; we should fulfil community needs; and we should design and produce locally-relevant learning materials that can fulfil local needs.

This is not, however, easy to do. First, there is the problem of defining specifically-local learning needs. Second, there is the problem of designing actual instructional materials. Third, there is the problem of producing those materials, howsoever crude they may be.

THE BRITISH COUNCIL PROJECT IN KENYA

Many years ago, the British Council had the same idea and they started a project with similar objectives within the Kenya national literacy programme. A few centres were started. Each was given stencil-making machines, duplicators, lettering sets and other supplies. Literacy teachers, supervisors and district adult education officers together produced some materials. The project was good as long as it lasted. The Department of Adult Education is continuing to initiate locally produced materials with some success.

LOCAL WRITING MAKES SENSE

Locally-written reading materials make much more sense than locally-made graphic materials. Locally-made tapes or videos are no more than a pipe dream in the Third World today.

Teachers and learners together can write useful materials based on individual experiences and on the oral history of the community. Once the group begins, considerable and varied talents may be discovered.

SHELL MATERIALS FOR LITERACY IN PAPUA NEW GUINEA

Papua New Guinea's shell books project should be of interest here. Papua New Guinea is committed to literacy in vernacular languages, that is, mother tongues. Once learned, literacy in the vernacular language must be practised and upgraded. Only then will it be sustainable. Only then will it be transferable to one of the national languages.

The problem is that Papua New Guinea has 869 languages by the latest count. It is, of course, impractical to produce from scratch indigenous materials in each of those languages. The shell books project is an effective compromise.

Two types of 'shell materials' are produced: resource shells (posters, graded booklets and games, with text in a national language) and blank shells (the same posters, booklets and games, but with no text; for shell books, the blanks are produced as 'picture pages').

When a community literacy worker in a particular language area identifies a topic of interest to the group, he or she requests a copy of the 'Resource Shell' on that topic. He also requests the required number of blank shells to be filled in with text in the local language.

The literacy worker then translates the text in the original resource shell into the local language. They type or write the translated text onto the stencils. Using silkscreen printers, they print the text onto the picture pages (that is, the blank shells). The new books are ready to fold, collate and cut.

Posters and games may not be needed in so many copies. Some may be printed. Some may be merely copied with pen or marker.

The shell books project warns people to be careful. It is important that shell materials supplement, not replace, local legends, poetry, songs and histories, or locally-produced awareness materials. Figures 6.2 to 6.5 provide examples of some shell materials.

THINGS TO DO OR THINK ABOUT

1. List the materials now in use in your literacy group. Are you satisfied with what you have for use with learners? Are you satisfied with what is available for teachers, such as a teacher's manual?

2. Do you know why the project or programme office has not produced a greater variety of materials? Is it a problem of funding resources? Is it a problem of non-availability of specialists to produce such materials? Is this because the curriculum is so organized that what you already have is considered sufficient?

3. List resources in the community that you had not thought of using before reading this chapter.

PREFACE

This is a *Shell Book.*
Shell Books are inexpensive and easy to produce
right in your village.

This book and many others are available without
any claim of copyright for non-profit translation
into vernacular languages.

For information contact:

The Shell Project
S.I.L. Box 398
Ukarumpa via Lae
PAPUA NEW GUINEA

Drawings by James Simon
Copyright 1990, S.I.L.

9

11

Figures 6.2 and 6.3

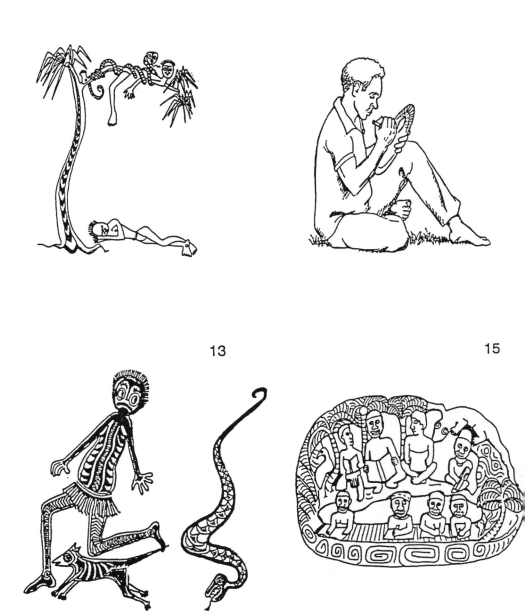

13

15

12

10

Figures 6.4 and 6.5

Chapter Seven

Understanding Learners and their Communities

Who are our learners? What are our learners like? What are their perceptions of the world? What are their motivations? What are their mental abilities?

Questions also arise regarding the communities where adults live. What is the community like – rural or urban or in-between? Are there few very rich people and many very poor people in the community? Who are the people with the most power, status and influence? Are community leaders in favour of literacy? If yes, how do they justify it? If not, why not?

Teachers must know their learners well. They should know these people with their particular hopes and desires. They should know their capacities to grow. They should also know the community. By knowing community leaders and their ideas, teachers will be able to make their programmes more effective.

The content of this chapter is the following:

- The psychology of learners

- The sociology and politics of communities

- Bringing it all together.

WORDS OF WISDOM AND VOICES FROM THE REAL WORLD

> To teach, the teacher must know both himself [or herself] and the learner. (Anonymous)

> The teacher who regards illiterates as ignorant and marginal commits 'a sin against the mind', feigning to disregard the fact that mere survival has caused such pupils to display tremendous character, intelligence and know-how and filled their minds with a culture of truth and knowledge. (Xie Xide in *Letters of Life*, Nathan/UNESCO, 1991)

It stands to reason that we should try to understand our learners. What makes them tick and what makes them move? What are their motivations? What are their attitudes towards learning? What is their history of learning? What problems do they think they have? What expectations do they have of teachers? What expectations do they have from literacy? What else is on their minds? In a general sense, what is their psychology of literacy learning?

It is also reasonable that we understand the kind of world our learners live in. The literacy we teach them they will have to practise in their real world – on their farms, in factories and in communities.

We can teach the farmer new agricultural skills. But does the farmer have land? Can the farmer get credit to buy better seeds and fertilizers? Is there a market for the farmer's produce? Similarly, we can teach the factory worker new skills of productivity. But will the employer share some of the gain from productivity with his workers?

Most important, new economic gains may also result in new social gains and a greater sense of self-esteem and power among the newly literate. Will others in the community like it? Will they resent it? What might they do about it?

The literacy teacher should also understand the community in relation to his or her own role. Which standards are acceptable in the community and which are not? Who can get things done? Who can make you feel unwelcome and who can make you leave? Who likes literacy work and who does not? In other words, we must understand the social, political and cultural structures of the communities in which they live.

The psychology of learners

WHAT IS PSYCHOLOGY AND HOW DOES IT AFFECT LEARNING?

At the beginning of this chapter, we listed things we should know about our learners. These were questions about the inner lives of our learners, the lives of their minds and their hearts.

In Table 7.1 we mention key psychological aspects of the human learner and then suggest briefly how learning might be affected:

The listing in is more or less haphazard. It covers aspects that can have consequences for classes and groups.

Table 7.1 Psychological characteristics and their relationship to learning

Psychological aspect(s)	Relation to learning
Ego, self-esteem	Individuals need to protect their egos, that is, they need self-esteem. Some egos can be very big. Ego clashes can result. Some people can not stand a joke and can not stand ridicule.
Habits	Individuals acquire particular Behaviours habits and behaviour patterns. These can be pleasant or unpleasant.
Motivation	Motivations have been discussed in detail elsewhere. Motivations determine what will move learners to learn or to act.
Perception	We do not see the world in the same way. Great misunderstandings can arise from different sets of perceptions.
Attitudes and values	Values about knowledge and attitudes to-wards learning and about people can enhance or block learning. Attitudes towards others such as women and minorities can be disruptive in groups.
Cognition and intelligence	Human abilities vary. Some are better with their hands, some are better with words. Some are more able than others in whatever they do.
Identity	People have a need to protect their ethnic and cultural identities. There can be serious trouble if identity is seen to be under attack, and feelings are hurt.

How do you understand your learners? We are not suggesting that after reading Table 7.1 you will become a psychologist and learn to understand your learners. Do not think that! These ideas are included to sharpen your sensibilities in your work with adults in classes. If you keep them in mind as you work with adults in your classes, you may become a sensitive teacher.

In the meantime, you should work with some general ideas:

Do not hurt your learner's self-esteem and do not get into ego clashes. You should not have a big head just because you are now a teacher. Do not think that by getting a teacher's job you have become superior to everyone else in the class. There will be people in your group with more experience, more knowledge and more wisdom than you. Never insult any learner. Do not ridicule people. If you want to make a joke, make a joke at your own expense.

Separate the person from performance. While giving feedback to your learners, be positive. Make them aware of what they have learned and not of what they have failed to learn. Separate the person from performance. A bad performance in reading does not make a person bad. A highly moral man may not know mathematics – yet!

Learn to read people's feelings and moods. Every day is not the same in the lives of people. Good things happen on some days. Some days are quite bad. People have different moods. They have different levels of energy. Be sensitive to this.

Accept people as people. Respect them for what they are. Develop a sense of togetherness in the group. Group solidarity is important.

What is political sociology and how does it affect learning?

Political sociology is a big expression! What it means is that you are able to understand the power structure in the community. You can learn a lot about the political sociology of a community by asking the following questions:

- Who is the most powerful person in the community? Where does his or her power come from?
- Who is economically dependent on whom?
- Who has the highest status? What is the source of his or her status?
- What people want change? What kind of change they want? Why?
- What people are interested in keeping things the way they are? Why?
- What are the myths, beliefs, values, rituals and ceremonies that keep things the way they are?

HOW DO THE POLITICS OF A COMMUNITY AFFECT LEARNING?

The politics of a community affect learning in many ways. First, the vested interests in a community may not even want a literacy programme to come into the community. Powerful people generally understand that literacy can empower those who are powerless. They know that distribution of knowledge through literacy will make people participants in their social, economic and political institutions.

Even if the first battle is won and a literacy programme comes into a community against the wishes of the powerful, there will be other influences. They will provide no support to the programme. They may actively subvert the programme. Employers may not give leave to workers to attend literacy classes. Landowners may not allow the teacher to visit landless labourers working on their estates. Finally, learners may see becoming literate as a hopeless task. They may find literacy to be 'useless'. They may find the political costs of attending literacy classes too high.

UNDERSTANDING YOUR COMMUNITIES AND USING YOUR UNDERSTANDING TO GOOD EFFECT

Again, we do not claim that the preceding discussion will make literacy teachers great political analysts. We do think, however, that it will make them sensitive to these issues.

To understand the community, teachers should go to the community. What the teachers do not understand themselves, they should try to learn from the people. Teachers must walk a very fine line, being careful to avoid being co-opted by powerful people in the community, yet without making these people their enemies.

Teachers should also remember that there are many powerful people in the world who want to use their power for good; their interests are not narrow interests, but wide enough to include progress and interests of many. When such is the case, teachers should get all the help possible from them.

Bringing it all together

How should a teacher bring it all together? How should a teacher make the best use of the psychology of learners and the politics of the community to get things done? The solution lies in building 'community resources'. This is done through participatory planning and collaborative action.

To succeed at the community level, the following four principles should be kept in mind:

1. Through participatory thinking, come up with collectively identified needs – development needs and learning needs.

2. Again, through participation and collaboration, let everyone share ownership of initiatives and projects.

3. Continue to learn and teach personal skills and skills for collaborative work.

4. Be efficient but flexible and creative in your management of the project.

THINGS TO DO OR THINK ABOUT

1. Do you know your learners as persons? Does knowing them as persons help you in knowing them as learners?

2. Do you think that you understand the community in which you work? If you wanted to assist a visitor to understand the community, what things would you point out to the visitor?

3. What resources will you call upon for community problem-solving and action? What leaders? What voluntary or government agencies?

Chapter Eight

Human Relations and the Dynamics of Teaching in Functional Literacy Groups

Can teachers succeed in teaching those they do not like? Will adult learners respect their literacy teachers if literacy teachers do not respect their learners? What are the effects of learners' feelings on learners' abilities to learn, on continuing to learn or dropping out, on failing or succeeding? How to organize instruction to enhance the pleasure of learning? How should the teacher keep a balance between authority and freedom?

This chapter argues that human relations are important for effective teaching and learning. We will also show that the teacher can manage instruction in the classroom in such a way that everyone learns better. These are important topics for teachers. They need to learn to examine their own social skills and to know how well they are managing the teaching–learning aspects of the class.

The discussion in this chapter will be presented in the following four parts:

- Cultural ecology of groups
- Groups as living systems
- Managing human relations
- Managing instructional dynamics within adult groups.

WORDS OF WISDOM AND VOICES FROM THE REAL WORLD

> Why do our teachers feel so superior?
> They behave as if we are ignorant fools
> As if we are little children.
> We are not empty pitchers.

We have minds of our own
We can reason things out
and, believe it or not,
we also have dignity.
(From a prose poem by Satyen Moitra, *Bengal Social Service
League, Calcutta, India*)

When all is said and done, the teaching of literacy is both a social process
and an instructional process. Before there is 'teaching', there has to be
'relating'. Human relations come first, instructional processes can happen later. Obviously, good human relations are most crucial to good
teaching.

Thus, in any group of adults where teaching–learning takes place,
these two processes take place at the same time. Human relations are
involved, since it is human beings that are interacting with each other,
and instructional strategies are involved, since teachers are trying to
assist in the learning of adults in their groups.

First, the drama of human relations within groups is enacted. The
stage, the plot, the roles and the costumes in this human relations drama
are all determined by the 'culture' of people. But in addition to a cultural
reality groups also have a reality in the present time. Groups, when they
come together, become 'living system'. The membership and the mood
of the members in living groups are the second layer of influence on
human relations in groups. It is within the context of these two influences
that instruction takes place.

Cultural ecology of groups

Cultural ecology is a fancy word with simple meanings. Culture is what
makes a Japanese, Japanese, and an Italian, Italian. Culture helps us
differentiate a Masai in East Africa from an Eskimo in northern Canada.

Ecology is another word for relations determined by the environment.
Cultural ecology is, therefore, that part of the climate in a classroom or
group which can be explained in terms of the culture or cultures of people
who have come together in a learner group.

To understand the cultural ecology of a group, we must know something about the following concrete aspects of the culture of group members:

Values, norms and taboos. The teacher must have a good idea of the values,
norms and taboos of people in the group. Values, norms and taboos, in

different ways, help people separate good from bad, and the ideal from the ordinary, and establish social and cultural do's and don't's.

Values, norms and taboos may relate, on the one hand, to such serious questions as free will, fatalism, personal duty, rights and social obligation. On the other hand, they may apply to avoidance of eating rabbits or eggs.

Patterns of social contact and relationships. The teacher must know about the group's acceptable patterns of social contact and social relationship. Muslim communities may have one set of such patterns and non-Muslim communities may have another. A Muslim community in Saudi Arabia will not have the same set of patterns as one in East African coastal villages.

Male culture, female culture. It is of some importance for literacy teachers to know what anthropologists have already learned, for instance that, within the same culture, the male subculture differs from the female subculture.

The functional literacy teacher needs to understand the general cultural ecology of the group to be able to handle human relations. One does not need a doctorate in anthropology to do that. What is required is sensitivity and goodwill. When in doubt – ask. Learn about the culture of groups from the group members – they are the experts. When you make a mistake, admit your ignorance and sincerely apologize.

Groups as living systems

Above, we discussed the cultural ecology of groups. Your groups will bring their cultural ecology with them to class.

But, as we indicated earlier, groups are also 'living systems'. Their immediate behaviour is determined by their membership. Who are the members? What are their ages, occupations, genders, social statuses, etc.? It is also determined by the present moods of group members – their worries, their angers and their anxieties. The physical states of group members – malnutrition and fatigue – also matter.

MEMBERS OF FUNCTIONAL LITERACY GROUPS

As we travel around the world, we come across a variety of groups of learners engaged in this wonderful and inspiring work of learning to read.

There can be all-men classes or all-women classes. Adult literacy groups are not always truly 'adult' groups. Quite often young children join literacy classes meant for adults. This is so because there are some rural areas in the Third World where adult classes have been opened but where elementary schools have not been reached yet. Young boys and girls therefore join adults in their classes. In many countries, mothers bring infants with them who sleep at their breasts while women learn. Classes, of course, also differ by urban and rural settings and by occupation.

Table 8.1 highlights various combinations that determine the particular climate of the living system called the literacy class.

Table 8.1 Various learner-group typographies

	Male Teacher	*Female Teacher*
All male adults	x	x
All male adults and young boys	x	x
All female adults	x	x
All female adults, young girls, and infants	x	x
Combined male and female	x	x
Combined male and female, boys and girls, and infants	x	x

These types of classes do indeed occur, depending upon cultures and conditions. Male teachers teach all-women classes, and mixed classes of males and females. Female teachers rarely teach such mixed classes. They are more likely to teach all-women classes. One reason is cultural; the other is that there simply are not enough female teachers to go around.

At times female teachers do teach classes with males and young boys. Fears about failures of such groups are unfounded. The kinds of problems that were anticipated by some people did not occur. Adults in communities are proud of their mothers, sisters and daughters taking up teaching jobs.

Female teachers typically do a good job of teaching other women. They have great patience with other women and do not lose patience with children who sometimes cry in classes. The same can not be said of male teachers who have to learn to be patient with mothers who come to class with infants in their laps.

It is in a living group that the cultural factors come into life. Learners with high social status in the community want special treatment within classes: some want to take over while some want to hide behind other people. All want to protect their egos. Some want to expand their egos at the cost of others.

People try to impose their views of right and wrong in general. They expect certain people to behave in a certain way within the group – especially, children, women and other disadvantaged groups. Living systems are a world of their own, complex and fascinating.

Managing human relations

People cannot learn human relations from books alone. They have to want to learn human relations in daily interactions. They have to practise and experiment. That means that they have to keep their eyes and ears open to watch for the effect they are having on other people. If they find people are embarrassed or offended, they have to apologize. Then they have to try again with greater sensitivity.

There are some general principles of human relations to be kept in mind:

1. *Have good intentions.* Good human relationships are built on the bed-rock of genuinely good intentions. Teachers have to be committed to work for the poor, the disadvantaged and the powerless.

2. *Have genuine respect for the people you are supposed to serve.* It is impor-tant that teachers have and show genuine respect for the people with whom they work. Teachers must respect their learners for what they are. They must respect their feelings and their ideas. Teachers must be democratic, treating everyone equally.

3. *Do group building, everyday.* Groups are not built once for ever. Main-taining a group is a continuous process. This means that the teacher will need to start every class session with some group-building remark or activity. The sharing of experiences can pro-vide the commonality on which to build further group work.

4. *Empathize.* Empathy is more than sympathy. To empathize means to put your self in somebody else's shoes and to see the world from their perspective. The teachers should ask the following questions. What would I be today, if I had been in the learner's place? What would I have done today, if I were the learner?

5. *Do not attribute.* To attribute means to decide to describe the feelings of others. 'You are angry!' 'You are insulting me!' 'You are jealous of me for my success!' These are all attributions. It is possible that the person is not angry but quiet because he is sick. It is possible that the person is not insulting but does not know enough English and has chosen the wrong word. It is possible that the person is not jealous, but does not have the social skills to say the right thing. The teacher must ask learners about their inner life rather than attributing and accusing them of certain feelings.

6. *Do not violate.* The teacher should not violate people's privacies or confidences.

7. *Do not ridicule.* Never ridicule the learners. This is particularly important in mixed groups of males and females with young children present. The consequences of ridicule and loss of face are felt outside the classroom and in the community.

8. *Emphasize the positive.* Learning is not easy. Learners will falter. They will make mistakes. It is important that the teacher emphasizes the positive. There should be no failures, only challenges to try again.

9. *Help people negotiate.* Learners in classes interact with and among each other. Many disagreements and clashes of wills arise. The teacher must learn to be an arbiter to negotiate differences among people.

10. *Heal, nurture and build.* What we are then asking from the teacher is that he or she be a healer, nurturer and builder of people. In helping others, the teacher, of course, helps himself or herself.

11. *Work toward personal bonding.* If there is success in the areas listed above, there will result what is called 'personal bonding' between the teacher and learners. They will become friends, even part of an extended family.

12. *Build group solidarity.* Inside the group, this leads to group solidarity. The teacher should strive for this.

13. *Teach others to learn human relations skills.* Teachers are not the only ones who should be sensitive and learn human relation skills. Others in the group should be taught also to learn human relations skills.

14. *Ask others to evaluate your human relations skills.* Ask adults in groups these three questions. What should I stop doing? What should I continue doing? What should I start doing? Teachers should have the courage to be judged by others before they judge them.

Managing instructional dynamics within adult groups

Literacy work is typically done with a teacher working with a group of fifteen to twenty-five learners. A most important aspect of the instructional dynamics in a literacy group is that a group is not homogeneous but may be composed of many subgroups within the larger group.

BIG GROUP, SMALL GROUP

The most important ability of a literacy teacher is to be able to recognize and then handle small groups within the larger group. Examine Figures 8.1 and 8.2 carefully.

The teacher should be able to establish each-one-teach-one groups, both inside and outside the class, so that adults who are ahead in reading and

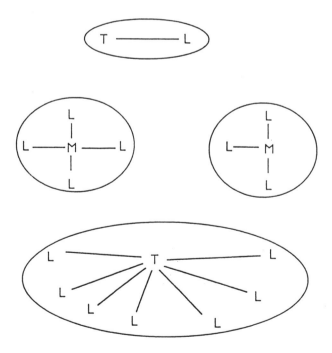

Figure 8.1 Different ways of organizing teaching and learning: each-one-teach-one; small groups of monitors and learners; and teacher in a large group. (T: teacher; M: monitor; L: learner)

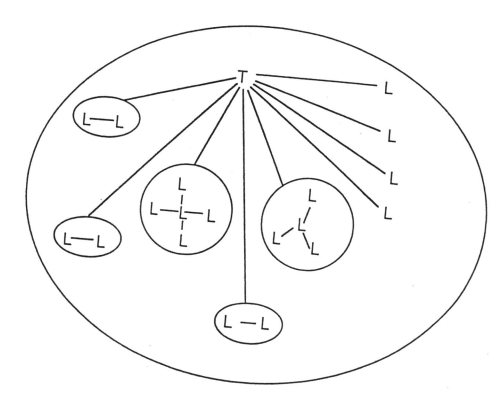

Figure 8.2 Different models of organizing teaching and learning within the same one class.
(*T: teacher; L: learner*)

writing help those who are somewhat behind. The teacher should be able
to choose monitors from among the larger group and establish small peer
groups of monitors–learners within the larger group. Thereafter the
teacher should be able to act as a manager of the total range of activities
taking place in the classroom. This can happen only if the following six
conditions are met.

1. *The class as a learning community*. The teacher should be able to emphasize the 'learning community' aspects of the group. All learners should be seen as resources.

2. *Teacher as coequal*. In this learning community, the teacher should be
   able to function as a co-equal without surrendering authority. The
   balance between teacher authority and solidarity with the group is
   important.

3. *Teacher as manager, not expert.* The teacher should see himself/herself as an instructional manager. The teacher may see himself/herself as being a step or two ahead, but not an expert authority. Teachers seldom know more than everybody else in their classrooms; teachers never know more than everybody put together! Teachers must, therefore, learn from learners. The teacher should be able be admit lack of knowledge when there is lack of knowledge. The teacher should then go to appropriate sources to find answers that the learners need and bring those answers to the learners.

4. *Plan learning together.* The teacher should engage in genuine participative planning of learning. Programmes and lessons should be planned together.

5. *Self-assessment procedures.* Along with participative planning, it is important that learners engage in self-assessment. Such self-assessment may include written tests, but must also include the learner's own satisfaction or dissatisfaction with progress.

6. *Help transfer knowledge for the world outside.* Finally, teachers must help learners connect with their classroom learning with the world outside. The dynamics of the classroom can be positively affected once learners know that their learning can be used in the real world.

THINGS TO DO OR THINK ABOUT

1. Ask your adult learners the following questions. What should I as a teacher continue doing? What should I as a teacher stop doing? What should I as a teacher start doing?

Thank them for their advice and think about what they say.

Chapter Nine

The Work of a Literacy Teacher

What are the essential tasks of a literacy teacher? The literacy teacher should, of course, teach literacy. But what else should the literacy teacher teach or do? Should the literacy teacher be responsible for teaching economic skills? Should the literacy teacher also teach political and cultural awareness? Are all these expectations realistic? Is there enough time for all these tasks to be performed?

The literacy teacher is more than a teacher of reading and writing. Of course, the literacy teacher often needs collaboration with an extension worker or the technician to teach functionality. But the functional literacy teacher has an important complementary part to play in teaching functionality.

In promoting awareness, once again the teacher needs help and support of others, but again his or her complementary role is most important.

The work of the literacy teacher goes farther than merely teaching in other important ways. For example, the functional literacy teacher is 'functionary' of the organization delivering literacy. Such an organization may be governmental or non-governmental, local or national. The teacher also becomes a local leader. Finally, the teacher is a development agent.

Teachers can learn a lot about themselves in this chapter. They will learn how they are viewed by others around them. This outsider's view will contribute to teachers' self-knowledge. Learning about other teachers in general will give teachers of adult literacy a sense of solidarity.

This chapter is divided into three sections:

- Literacy teachers as people and professionals
- The multiple roles of a literacy teacher
- The worth of it all; rewards that money cannot buy.

WORDS OF WISDOM AND VOICES FROM THE REAL WORLD

> Since the literacy and health workers are for the most part younger men [and women], they do not have authority in their own right to influence the people substantially. Headmen lend their prestige to persuade the community to accept and follow the new information which the teachers wish to share. They also provide the suitable manpower to share the work load, as well as make the programmes effective in the communities. (From a report on the 'Literacy and Health Training' programme in Ketengban, Indonesia, printed in the Summer Institute of Linguistics' Annual Report, 1990)

There are real people behind roles and designations. As people come to work, they bring their personal needs, aspirations and personalities with them.

In anticipating the personal needs, aspirations and personalities of literacy teachers, we will talk generally about literacy teachers as people and as professionals.

Literacy teachers as people and professionals

Literacy work all around the world is unstructured and underfunded. By unstructured we mean that we do not have a system for adult education as we often have for the education of young children. Only a few countries have any permanent institutions of adult education and adult literacy.

Funding patterns for adult education and adult literacy are also uncertain, and go up and down from year to year depending upon the political climate. Actual funds dedicated to adult education are almost always inadequate.

LITERACY TEACHING IS A PART-TIME PROFESSION

Literacy work almost everywhere in the world is part-time work, usually done in the evening when farmers and workers are back home from a full day's work.

Women's classes in the rural areas of the Third World are now beginning to be organized during early afternoons when the women's morning work is over and when cooking of the evening meal has not yet started. Of course, literacy work with women is also considered part-time work.

It is only in countries such as China where adult education and adult literacy is moving towards becoming full-time work. This is possible because China has institutionalized adult education. In other words, special institutions of adult education and adult literacy have been established. All adult education and adult literacy work has been brought into these institutions, called peasants' schools of culture and technology. Full-time teachers have been appointed to work in these institutions.

Botswana also has some full-time supervisors for adult education and adult literacy work at the district level, but no full-time literacy teachers.

LITERACY TEACHING IS VOLUNTARY WORK

Literacy work is seen not only around the world as part-time but is expected to be done by the people for the people voluntarily. It is seldom purely voluntary, though. A small honorarium is typically promised – but by no means regularly paid. The amount of honorarium may often be as low as 2 to 3 dollars a month.

Volunteers are sought from among university and college students and sometimes from secondary-school students. This seldom works because volunteers are needed in villages, which is not where the students live. They live in towns.

Also, students in the university, colleges and higher secondary schools want to do volunteer work only during their vacation periods and not throughout the year. Only in Cuba, Somalia and Nicaragua were students asked to volunteer for long periods of time. Schools were closed so that students could go into the villages, live among the people and teach them literacy for development.

Typically, volunteers for literacy teaching come from within the communities in which literacy work is done, or they come from communities nearby. This is true in both rural and urban areas.

LITERACY TEACHERS: IDENTITY AND SOCIAL CLASS

Most literacy teachers work in the rural areas of the Third World where most of the illiterate people live. Most are young school leavers who have finished elementary education but have not gone on to secondary education. In other words, they have completed elementary school but have not been able to win a seat in a higher secondary school. In the process they have been stamped as 'failures' by the educational establishment.

Often these school-leavers-turned-literacy-teachers are in the villages because they have nowhere else to go – they belong to a social class that can neither pull its weight within the education system nor within the world of work and they know that their elementary education will not get them a job in the city. The only economic opportunity in the community is subsistence farming. Thus, most of them stay in their communities as reluctant farmers.

For most of them, therefore, to teach part-time in a literacy programme is an opportunity to do something worthwhile. It is a window of hope which may provide some social and economic mobility. In fact, in the United Republic of Tanzania literacy teachers after some years of teaching got opportunities to continue their education at secondary schools or at junior teacher-training colleges. This proved to be an important incentive for volunteer teachers.

The multiple roles of a literacy teacher

The tasks of a literacy teacher are many. There are at least three intertwined roles: the role of a teacher, the role of a development agent within the community and the role of a functionary of the government.

Let us look at some of the things that an effective teacher does.

BEFORE THE START OF A LITERACY GROUP

Literacy programmes typically train their teachers a few weeks or months ahead of the date when a literacy project will be launched. On return to their communities, trained literacy teachers are expected to do a lot.

INFORM AND MOBILIZE THE COMMUNITY

The teacher is expected to go around in the community and spread information in the community about the literacy programme to be implemented. The teacher, of course, has to be well-informed in order to answer questions.

Information and mobilization go together. But mobilization involves more than merely spreading information. Mobilization involves informing, influencing and persuading all together.

Working with extension workers. The teacher has to enlist the help of local leaders as well as other extension workers in the community. Fortunately, extension workers are now more sympathetic to literacy work. After years of extension work with illiterate people, they have come to understand the limits of success of agricultural and health extension with illiterate people. They know that literacy work helps extension work. Literacy teachers will have to network with the extension workers and get their help in the mobilization process.

Working with community leaders. Too often community leaders are taken for granted. We assume that as community leaders, they must be for the development of the communities and that they welcome all literacy and development work. That need not be so. It is possible that community leaders are not convinced of the usefulness of literacy work. Others may feel threatened by the unknown. They may ask: 'What might it mean to have literacy in the community?' Some may refuse to be involved; some may work actively against literacy. The literacy teacher has to find out what different leaders are thinking and why. He or she has then to deal with existing realities. If local leaders are not co-operative, followers in the community will have to be educated to understand their interests. Furthermore, help will need to be sought from the upper layers of leadership.

CONDUCTING QUICK INFORMAL COMMUNITY SURVEYS

After returning from the training site to the community, the literacy teacher should conduct quick and informal community surveys. The questions in such surveys should be quite simple; the answers will be most important.

The survey should seek answers to questions such as: How many illiterate people are there in the community? How many are male and how many are female? Who among them is ready to join the literacy class? Would they be willing to come to mixed classes of men and women? What would be the best time in the year for starting a literacy class? What would be the best location for a literacy class? What should be the frequency, duration and time for the literacy class? What expectations would they have of the literacy class? What uses do they expect to make of literacy skills?

These quick and informal surveys should be used to ascertain learners' needs in regard to levels of literacy skills, uses of literacy and needs in terms of food, health and childcare. The specimen of a village survey form (Figure 9.1) is from Malawi.

VILLAGE PROFILE

1. Number of people in the village   male............................
   - female........................
   - total..........................

2. Illiterates aged 15 years +   male............................
   - female........................
   - total..........................

3. Crops grown in the area (according to importance)
   - (i)...
   - (ii)..
   - (iii)...
   - (iv)...

4. Other occupations in the village:
   - farming (farming animals)   yes/no
   - fishing   yes/no
   - others (name)...

5. Extension agents paying visits to your village:
   - Agriculture extension agents.............................
   - Health extension agents...................................
   - Others..

6. Development activities in the village (name)
   ....

7. Number of classes in the village...

8. Number of learners   male...
   - female..

9. Village Literacy Committee (if present): list members
   ....
   ....

10. Literature/books found in the village:

	yes	no
Boma Lathu (newspaper)	....	....
farmers' magazine	....	....
Malawi News	....	....
Odini (newspaper)	....	....
others (name)		

11. Number of radios in the village:
   - Donated by the Government..
   - Owned by people:...

Figure 9.1

SELECTING LEARNERS FOR LITERACY GROUPS

In some communities, there are more people who want to learn to read and write than can be accommodated in literacy classes. This was a typical problem in the rural areas of Malawi during the 1980s. In such a case, the literacy teacher may be asked to assist in learner selection.

Selection criteria. Typical criteria in many countries for learner selection are the productive age in regard to the economic contributions. Adults in the age range of 18–35 or 18–45 are given preference because they are active in the economy and will be able to use what they learn from functional literacy programmes to improve their productivity on the farm or in the factory.

Learner selection, at least in part, always remains a political problem. The literacy teacher should assist and do his or her best to apply selection criteria fairly, avoiding taking over the whole burden of decision-making. Let community leaders decide.

Celebrating opening of classes. It is nice to have a celebration marking the opening of the class. Everyone should be invited. This is a time to let children, family members and friends in the community participate. It is time to get affirmation.

WHEN CLASSES BEGIN

Once classes begin, the essential task of the literacy worker begins – to teach functional literacy to adult groups.

CLASSROOM TEACHING

In the various chapters of this practical guide, we have discussed the methodologies of teaching, utilization of materials, and the social and educational dynamics of groups. Here we only remind teachers that their tasks involve group formation, motivating, teaching, reviewing and evaluating.

Earlier, we discussed how a literacy teacher might discover purely local learning needs of learners in the group. We then suggested how some materials could be locally produced to meet those local needs. Please review that material at this time.

MAINTAINING TEACHING–LEARNING

In a sense starting a literacy group is easier than keeping it going. When a literacy project begins, there is always some effort directed towards the mobilization of both learners and teachers. Local leaders help. Some outsiders come in to influence and inspire. But once classes begin, the teacher and the learners are left to themselves. If there is no continuous maintenance of the class by the teacher, classes wither away.

Handling absenteeism. Learners who begin to be frequently absent must be met in the fields or at their homes. Those who drop out must be persuaded to come back. Everyone must be helped by way of emotional support and in terms of help in learning to read. The literacy teacher may not be able to do it all alone and the assistance of others in the class should be sought. Local literacy committees should help as should extension workers.

Self-evaluation by learners as a motivational device. There is a deeper layer involved in the maintenance of literacy classes. Learners must be assisted in conducting self-evaluations. They should learn to evaluate their progress or lack of progress. If they are impatient, they should learn to be patient. If they are too complacent, they should be helped to move along so that they can experience achievement.

Connecting learning with outside environment. More important, as part of the maintenance of literacy classes, teachers should continue pointing out the connections between what adults learn in class and the world outside the classroom. Adults should be made aware of the fact that there are words and numbers surrounding us wherever we are. All human environments have become literate environments. There is writing in the Kalahari desert, on the Himalayas and in the depth of the seas. Closer to home, there is writing on tea bags, medicine bottles and bags of seeds.

PROMOTING PARTICIPATORY LEARNING

To keep classes going, the adults must stay involved. For real learning to occur, they must take responsibility for their own learning.

Boydell and Pedlar, two American authors, explain how participatory learning can be promoted by creating 'learning communities'.

Learning communities, they tell us, are based on two interrelated principles. First, each member of the learner group takes the primary responsibility for identifying and meeting his or her own learning needs and second each member of the learner group takes the responsibility for helping each of the others in identifying and meeting his or her learning needs, and offers to act as a resource person to the learning community.

The above can be accomplished if the teacher can: (a) build the climate by developing openness, interdependence and mutuality; (b) create a climate for sharing needs; (c) provide resources; (d) encourage co-operative planning; and (e) engage in participative evaluation.

EVALUATION OF LEARNER'S ACHIEVEMENT

The literacy teacher has to play an important role in evaluating achievement of adult learners in classes or groups. This type of evaluation is needed for diagnostic and evaluative purposes.

The teacher has to conduct evaluation of learner achievements to diagnose problems and difficulties. Based on such a diagnosis, the teacher will be able to improve his or her own teaching.

The other purpose of evaluation is to find out how much and how well adults have learned at a particular time in the life of a programme. That would be an evaluative use.

Evaluation can be of various kinds. Each serves different purposes.

Self-evaluation. Self-evaluation as the name suggests is conducted by the learner. Tests may be self-administered and compared with answers provided in the primer or book. This is typically done in correspondence courses.

For qualitative self-evaluation, the teacher can act as the sounding board. The learner may establish his or her own criteria of success and satisfaction. The learner can conduct his or her own evaluation. The teacher can provide reinforcement or encouragement towards higher achievement.

The positive aspects of self-evaluation are obvious, but so too are the limitations. Results of self-administered tests remain private. No public record is formed. And comparisons according to a norm (standard yardstick) are not possible. In regard to such comparisons, qualitative self-evaluation is even more ambiguous.

Participative evaluation. This is an evaluation which is more learning than evaluating. Adults in a group, together with everyone else, establish criteria and standards of success. They make statements about the impact of a programme on their lives. The teacher simply creates conditions under which participative evaluation can take place. Participative evaluation uses existing reports and records and leaves in its wake reports and records.

Testing for achievement. Testing for achievement means administering tests often made by the project but sometimes by the teacher. These tests typically concern reading, writing and numeracy. Even when functionality and awareness are taught, they are seldom tested. Functionality and awareness tests are only made in some rare experimental programmes .

In the pages that follow examples of tests for field-level use by teachers are included. Teachers can compare them with tests in their own programme or to make their own tests.

EVALUATION OF THE IMPACT OF FUNCTIONAL LITERACY

Functional literacy is supposed to change the personal lives of individuals and the quality of life in communities. Impact evaluation is intended to determine the extent of such changes.

Literacy teachers are not expected to do systematic impact evaluation on their own, but there is no reason why teachers should not keep their eyes open to see how adults in their groups might be changing in subtle or direct ways. They should note the uses people make of literacy in their daily lives. They should look out for the effects of adult literacy on family life, on churches, on school attendance and on innovations in agriculture and nutrition.

This will be mostly anecdotal data, but there is nothing wrong with anecdotal data that show changes. Such items will be excellent candidates for entries in a teacher's journal and for class discussion.

Teachers may also be required to assist in more systematic 'impact evaluation' conducted by the headquarters. They may have to assist in selecting communities, careful samples of farmers and their spouses, and actually administering interviews and conducting observations and tests.

BEING A FUNCTIONARY OF THE TOTAL LITERACY SYSTEM

In addition to being a teacher and evaluator, the literacy teacher also has to act as a functionary of the larger literacy project, programme or campaign.

That means, at least, being available to work with other functionaries who come to visit from the ward, zonal or district levels. The teacher will have to be the bridge between the visitors, and local leaders and learners.

A most important function of the literacy teacher is to keep records of functional literacy activities. Two types of records are recommended: an attendance register and a teacher's journal. All literacy programmes have an attendance register of some sort. The teacher's journal is not, however, that common.

In discussing the evaluation role of the teacher, special reference was made to the teacher's journal as an evaluation tool.

We would now like to refer to the attendance register. We could easily have discussed the attendance register also as an evaluation tool, but it is first and foremost a record. It is a record of learner attendance and of the teacher's work. Hence it is discussed here as a separate instrument of the teacher as a functionary.

Figure 9.2 shows a typical attendance register from the functional literacy programme in Malawi. The register can deliver a considerable amount of information on the day-to-day life of the class.

After some initial training, one can work out from such a register descriptive information on the life of a literacy class:

1. Attendance ratios by day / week / month.

2. Attendance ratios overall / by gender / by age groups

3. Fluctuations of attendance over time

4. Reasons stated for non-attendance

5. Dropout ratios and patterns

6. Progress in terms of lessons covered.

Data from the attendance register provide a solid foundation for a management information system for the total literacy project.

DEVELOPMENT AGENT ROLE: NETWORKING WITH EXTENSION WORKERS

Functional literacy is literacy plus functionality plus awareness. Literacy classes take care of the literacy component and offer preliminary ideas on functionality and awareness. But that is never enough. Both functionality and awareness require separate and more substantive attention.

INCOME-GENERATION PROJECTS

Some functional content is taught within the literacy class. Some additional knowledge and skills are taught through various series of demonstrations organized for the class or the community. A series of demonstrations may be arranged on baby care, on nutritious cooking, on pest control through pesticides, on seed selection or on making ridges for cotton farming.

Functional literacy projects today are complementing teaching of functionality with the actual organization of 'income generation projects'. Income generation projects are projects meant to generate real income. They are planned, implemented and managed by learners, with the help and guidance of literacy teachers and extension agents. Learners earn some income as they learn to become entrepreneurs. Projects may

ATTENDANCE REGISTER

Month: .... Year: ....

Number of learners at the beginning of the month: ....

Number of lessons taught ....

Date class held																									
Lesson																								Number of days learners attended classes	Number of learners tested
Names of learners																									

Figure 9.2 Attendance register from the Malawi fundamental literacy programme

include: poultry farming, flour mill, bakery, beer brewing, sewing, brick making, basket making, pottery, etc.

Often these income-generating activities are open to the whole community and not limited to literacy learners. In doing so, care must be taken to see that the income-generating project and its income are not captured by a few in the village who already have money and power.

The objectives of income-generating projects are more than merely the learning of economic skills. People learn management and financial accounting. Indeed, participants in income-generating projects often demand that they be taught accounting and management skills.

NETWORKING WITH EXTENSION AGENTS

Income-generating projects can rarely be done by teachers alone. Typically teachers would neither have the time nor the capacity to help learners establish an income-generating project.

This is where networking with the extension workers becomes crucial. Everywhere in the Third World, there are extension workers busy teaching people new techniques of agriculture, cattle raising, horticulture, and so forth. Home science and crafts are being taught as well. Thus there is sure to be somebody in the community who can help the teacher to get started.

If there is already an ongoing income-generating project in the community, then the task is different. Then the teacher's task is to integrate the class with the income-generating activity. Income-generating projects generate income which is distributed among members. An on-going project may not be willing to let new people join in. In such a case an alternative or ancillary project may have to be organized.

AWARENESS OF LEARNERS AND OF TEACHERS

Awareness is the hardest thing to teach in functional literacy classes. Teachers themselves can not always be assumed to have acquired awareness.

Content of awareness is also political. It involves explanations of the human condition. Why are some people rich and many poor? Where is the power to make decisions? Who makes decisions? What people are favoured by those decisions? What can be done by the common people to guard their own interests? Here the literacy teacher may want to make connections with political leaders of different persuasions and have them speak to literacy groups.

The most important source of materials for promoting awareness are the newspaper, radio and television. Topics from these media can be discussed in study circles and other kinds of discussion groups. Elsewhere, we have provided brief hints on how such study circles might be organized.

POST-LITERACY ACTIVITIES

Even as a literacy teacher starts teaching a literacy class, he or she should begin to think in terms of post-literacy activities.

ANTICIPATING THE POST-LITERACY PHASE

The teacher should begin to plan for post-literacy work even while adults are beginning to learn to read and write. Learners who think in this larger perspective will be more likely to stay in the group, to retain and use their literacy skills.

As the literacy class goes through its phase of four to six months, the literacy teacher should bring the learners into touch with the print resources already in the community. This may mean bringing a newspaper to class or borrowing a book from a library or a friend and bringing it to class.

If there is no library in the village, efforts should be made to start a rural library. This library can be a mobile library which can be stored in a tin box of some sort and move from place to place.

WORKING IN A POST-LITERACY PROGRAMME

Very soon some teachers may be working not with literacy classes but with post-literacy groups. This is already happening in many countries, the United Republic of Tanzania for instance.

In most places 'post-literacy' is conceptualized as a higher level of literacy. This is an obvious second chance for adults to complete elementary education missed as children. This means in the United Republic of Tanzania, for example, that post-literacy teaching is handled in clearly-defined levels that run parallel with grades in elementary education. In Ethiopia, post-literacy is similarly conceptualized.

In theory, at least, post-literacy training can be conceptualized to include acquisition of higher literacy skills and learning to use literacy to solve day-to-day problems of life and work, relating to economic functionality and civic awareness. Most important, in the post-literacy stage one must acquire both depth and breadth as a reader, and become an independent consumer and producer of information.

The best method of post-literacy teaching is discussion within the context of a study circle organized at, for instance, the community library.

TEACHER BURN-OUT, TEACHER LIGHT-UP

Our description of the work of a literacy teacher may be beginning to look like an impossible task. It is not impossible, but it is definitely highly demanding. The trouble is that literacy programmes demand a lot from their volunteer teachers and offer them little in return. They pay very small honoraria and unfortunately do not even offer social rewards.

It is no wonder that there is often as much teacher drop-out within literacy projects as there is learner drop-out. Teachers feel neglected, alone, unrewarded and unappreciated. Some who do not drop-out, burn-out. They lose interest in what they are doing. They go through the motions without really helping learners. They lose their effectiveness.

There are some things that must be done for literacy teachers of adults among them: occasional in-service training workshops, organized study tours and recognition by learners, community leaders and colleagues. This will light-up their working lives.

The worthwhileness of it all: rewards that money can not buy

Literacy teachers as we have said repeatedly are, typically, volunteers. They are low-paid. But they do have opportunities to grow and gain. We do need to look at the positive side.

PART OF SOMETHING GREATER THAN THEMSELVES

Literacy teachers must know that they are a part of something greater than the literacy class in which they teach. They are part of a national movement, in fact of an international movement. They are the implementers of their nation's development mission.

PROFESSIONAL KNOWLEDGE, SOCIAL EXPERIENCE

First through training and then through day-to-day work teachers acquire valuable professional knowledge of teaching and organization. They also learn subject matter knowledge of science, technology, agriculture, health and family planning.

They acquire considerable experience in working with other people in a variety of social settings as well as useful knowledge about the community, about youth and adults, about human relations, and about leadership and followership. This is like going to a rural university!

ECONOMIC GAINS

Literacy teachers seldom get a sufficient stipend, but they do acquire economic knowledge, especially within functional literacy projects. Functional literacy teachers have been known to avail themselves of this economic knowledge, sometimes starting small businesses for themselves or their families. They also gain from the income-generating projects established within functional literacy projects.

STATUS IMPROVEMENT IN THE COMMUNITY

The gains in the social status of literacy teachers are always high. People in the community start calling them 'Teacher!' They begin to get invited to functions and parties. Many literacy teachers have been known to acquire positions of political influence. That is not bad!

THINGS TO DO OR THINK ABOUT

1. Do you play all the roles that we have discussed teacher, evaluator, functionary and development agent?

2. How many of the above roles do you play well? Explain.

3. Which of the above roles do you enjoy the most? Which ones the least?

4. What kinds of changes you think are necessary to enable literacy teachers to play all of these roles at some level of satisfaction.

Chapter Ten

The Literacy Supervisor in Action

What is the role of the supervisor in relation to the literacy teacher? Is the supervisor an inspector? Is the supervisor a professional colleague of the teacher, a professional consultant? Is the supervisor a teacher's helper and friend?

What is the role of a supervisor in the community? Is the supervisor a mobilizer, a community organizer, a development agent?

We suggest that the supervisor is all of the above. The supervisor has to both guide and direct the work of the teacher, to inspect the teacher's work and provide mentoring to the teacher, thereby helping in the teacher's personal growth. A supervisor is indeed the teacher's teacher, a community organizer and a development agent.

Teachers should be interested in knowing about the supervisor's role, as this will tell them what to expect from the supervisor and enable them to team up with the supervisor in order to do important things together for adult learners and the community.

This chapter focuses on the supervisor of literacy teachers. The discussion is presented under eight headings.

- The role and functions of the literacy supervisor
- The supervisor as a functionary
- The supervisor as a development agent
- The supervisor as a community organizer and a builder of networks
- The supervisor as a literacy specialist
- The supervisor as a trainer
- The supervisor as a mentor
- The supervisor as an evaluator.

WORDS OF WISDOM AND VOICES FROM THE REAL WORLD

They come.

They sit.

They talk.

They eat.

They leave.

(A disappointed field worker talking about supervisors and other officials visiting from the headquarters)

The role and functions of the literacy supervisor

There is more than one designation for the person who supervises literacy work in the field. Literacy supervisor, literacy assistant and literacy co-ordinator are some of the names used in Third World literacy programmes.

The literacy supervisor is generally a full-time employee of a project, although sometimes school headmasters are requested to supervise literacy classes run for adults in their area.

The literacy supervisor is the person in the middle. On one side are the grassroots workers in the field, on the other the administrators, specialists, planners and policy-makers in the upper levels of a literacy project, programme or campaign (see Figure 10.1).

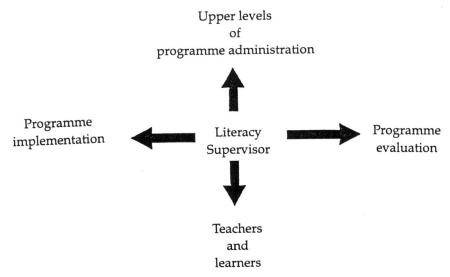

Figure 10.1 The literacy supervisor as the person in the middle
Computer graphic by Kenichi Kubota, 1991

Responsibility. A literacy supervisor may supervise the work of as many as thirty to fifty literacy centres spread over twenty to thirty contiguous villages. If literacy supervisors can be supplied with motorized transportation, their outreach can expanded to twice as much.

In Indonesia, a *Penilik* (supervisor) at the sub-district level may supervise 100 different programmes (not just classes) in as many as twenty villages. This raises questions both of time and ability. The *Penilik* may not have the ability to monitor so many different groups with different income-generating activities.

The literacy supervisor is a person in the middle in another sense, standing between implementation and evaluation. He or she helps with the programme and also evaluates its results. Thus, the literacy supervisor is a real educational administrator, implementing the literacy programme in the area with efficiency, as well as an educator, ensuring that the objectives of the literacy programme are being achieved.

GETTING READY FOR THE VISIT

The supervisor must come to the community ready for the visit in order to make the best use of the opportunity. Before departing on a field trip, the supervisor should have thought about the following: (1) materials to take along for the teacher, the learners and community leaders, such as chalk, additional copies of primers, teacher's guides, tests and forms, newspapers, and magazines, tapes, etc.; (2) team-building by bringing ideas from teachers in other villages to the teacher in this particular community (what did the supervisor see in earlier visits to other communities that is worth mentioning and discussing with this particular teacher?); (3) community organization and networking (what, when, with whom and how?); (4) class visit and teacher orientation (what difficulties were seen during the last visit and what advice was given?); and (5) gathering feedback and data collection in the class and the community.

The supervisor as functionary

First and foremost, the supervisor is seen by the teacher and the community as a functionary of the literacy project.

SUPERVISOR AS BOSS? SUPERVISOR AS INSPECTOR?

Ideally, the supervisor is neither the boss nor the inspector. Unfortunately, that does not stop the community from seeing the supervisor as the boss of the literacy teacher. The supervisor is the person whom they use to carry their complaints and satisfactions about the programme to the higher officials and organizers. The supervisor is, therefore, seen as powerful.

Too often, the teacher also views the supervisor in the image of the school inspector. Teachers hide problems from the supervisor for fear of being held responsible for those problems; some are truly afraid of supervisors.

Supervisors, of course, often act as bosses and inspectors. As official visitors from the outside, they exercise power and some enjoy this. They sometimes treat teachers and learners badly.

PUTTING THE SUPERVISOR ROLE IN PERSPECTIVE

It is important that the role of the supervisor be discussed as part of training of both teachers and supervisors. Some of the training of supervisors and teachers may be conducted together for this purpose.

More important, supervisors should not simply be sent to communities with their particular charge to do literacy work. Supervisors should be personally introduced to the community by their higher officers or appropriate local community leaders. At this time the supervisors' role and functions, and their duties and responsibilities should be explained to teachers, learners and the community.

The supervisor as a development agent

Literacy means the development of individual men and women. Literacy brings development to communities and societies. Thus, everyone working in literacy and functional literacy projects, programmes and campaigns is by definition a development agent. This includes literacy supervisors who, since they often work in thirty to fifty contiguous communities, have a broader perspective than that of individual teachers spread over different communities.

Literacy supervisors should be aware of their role as development agents. That means that they should plan and manage their literacy work within the context of development.

Planning and managing 'literacy for development'. This would mean that a supervisor should look at the development picture as a whole in the particular area under his or her charge and ascertain the following:

- What problems are shared across villages?
- What solutions can be shared across villages?
- What resources can be shared across villages?

- What instructional materials can be produced for use in all or almost all of the classes in the area?

- How can all the villages co-operate in mobilization for literacy work?

- How can all villages learn from each other to put literacy to use in development?

The supervisor as a community organizer and a builder of networks

During visits to a particular community, a supervisor can also help in community organizing. Networking among literacy workers, school teachers and extension workers should also be done. In both cases, however, there are limits.

A supervisor is responsible for many communities and therefore does not live within the community being supervised. Thus the supervisor visits infrequently. However hard supervisors may try, people see them as outsiders. This has both advantages and disadvantages. It is difficult to establish good rapport – rapport, that mix of friendship and understanding, is better when one lives in the community. This difficulty hinders good community organization and networking.

There are advantages. The supervisor is seen as an outsider and as a person in authority. Since the supervisor comes infrequently, he or she is also given greater attention. That assists in establishing meetings with community leaders, organizing functions, and in meeting other educators and extension workers in the field. All these people are considerate to the visitor.

In most parts of the world, literacy supervisors stay overnight in the communities they visit. Farmers come home in the evenings and after the supervisor has talked to farmers it is too late to go back. In fact, there is no means of transportation to go back. There is nothing available.

In some projects, in Botswana for example, supervisors are given motor cycles to visit communities. This has increased the frequency of visits to villages. Ironically, overnight stays in communities have almost disappeared. The motor cycle has made it easy to come, but it has also made it easy to leave! This is unfortunate. As far as possible, supervisors should stay overnight in the communities. They should take advantage of their overnight stay to talk to learners and community learners. During each and every visit, the supervisor should plan on doing community organizing and networking. Both require continuous work.

The supervisor as a literacy specialist

The literacy supervisor is almost always seen as being a literacy specialist. The supervisor seldom fails to visit the literacy teacher inside the literacy class and to observe the teacher while teaching. That is indeed how it should be. The supervisor should be well-versed in the methodology of teaching reading, writing and numeracy. The supervisor should be familiar with the literacy materials in use in the class.

THE NECESSITY OF DIAGNOSTIC KNOWLEDGE

Familiarity with teaching methods and instructional materials is not sufficient. It is essential that the supervisor should have diagnostic knowledge about the teaching and learning of literacy.

Diagnostic knowledge helps the supervisor diagnose problems just as a doctor diagnoses a health problem. This means that while observing the class, the supervisor should be able to see both the good and the bad, both the strengths and the weaknesses. The supervisor should be able to identify the problems of social relations in the class and the problems of teaching–learning in the class. At the same time, the supervisor should be able to record the successes in learning and working together.

Again, the supervisor should be able to distinguish between the specific problems of that day and general problems that might be encountered regularly, even daily.

AN OBSERVATION INVENTORY FOR THE SUPERVISOR

The supervisor should use some sort of instrument or tool to make notes on the following questions:

- Is the location and accommodation of the class adequate?
- Is the classroom well lit and well ventilated?
- How is the seating in the class organized? Are all women sitting in the last few rows?
- Is the chalkboard hanging at the right place and is it well-painted and clean?
- Are the appropriate wall charts properly displayed?
- Do all the learners have books of their own to read?
- Is reading a whole-group activity? If so, is everyone at the same page and following the instructions?
- Is the teacher polite?

- Does the teacher depend on only one or two people in the group to answer his or her questions?
- Does the teacher keep everyone's interest?
- Does the teacher ask analytical questions?
- Does the teacher make people think for themselves?
- Is the teacher able to judge if individual learners and the group as a whole are learning?
- Is the teacher able to diagnose learning problems?
- Is the teacher able to adapt to learners' needs, i.e. repeat part of the lesson, conduct drill or break class into subgroups for peer group assistance?

Such an inventory will help supervisors in two ways. First, it will help them discuss the details of the visit with the teachers. Second, it will help them keep a record of visits and build upon this during subsequent visits. In addition to this observational data, supervisors should also collect qualitative data by talking informally with learners and others in the community. This is absolutely essential for getting a good picture of what is going on. Suggestions for doing this can be found below in the section dealing with 'The supervisor as evaluator' (p. 153).

The supervisor as a trainer

Supervisors play an important role in the training of literacy teachers in both pre-service and in-service training phases. Supervisors often join other specialists in lecturing and demonstrating in pre-service teacher-training courses. Many short-term in-service teacher training courses are given by supervisors independently.

There is yet another type of training that the supervisor provides to the teacher during the supervisor's visit to the teacher's class and community. This is on-going concrete training. This training is tailor-made to fit the exact needs of a particular literacy teacher.

This kind of training is 'training by example' and 'training in action'. It could cover all the aspects of community organization, class organization, human relations with leaders and learners, teaching reading and writing, communication and networking, record keeping and handling of data for evaluation.

Both the supervisor and the teacher should be aware of this opportunity for training and must make the best use of such an opportunity. This means that the supervisor has to 'think aloud' for the teacher to know and understand what is going through the mind of the supervisor.

The supervisor as a mentor

Mentoring is a word much used today in education and business. Mentor means a wise and trusted teacher or guide. Mentoring, therefore, means training and guiding a student or a fresh colleague patiently, wisely, in a context of mutual trust. For the literacy supervisor, it will mean being a senior colleague of the literacy teacher, not a boss, not an inspector.

The ability of the supervisor to mentor has serious consequences for the literacy programme at the grassroots. Literacy teachers almost everywhere in the world work hard and long hours for very little reward. Supervisors have to give them non-monetary rewards that are part of a mentoring relationship. It is the supervisor who can say 'Thank you!' to the teacher on behalf of the project.

Supervisors have to help their teachers grow as people and professionals. They have to make them feel important. It is only through this sort of mentoring that teacher burn-out or teacher drop-out will decrease. Teacher morale will increase and this will have good effects on learners.

The supervisor as an evaluator

The role of the supervisor in 'information gathering' and 'evaluation' may be second only to the role of mentoring.

The supervisor can play a most significant role in information gathering. This will include two categories of information:

Descriptive information is the information developed from data generated in the very process of implementing a programme. Nothing special needs to be done except for adding and tabulating available data. Such data may relate to the number of adults in class, their sex and age, rates of absenteeism, drop-out, and so forth. Descriptive information may also be developed from scores on tests of reading and writing.

Evaluative information is developed for evaluative purposes. It can be of two types:

Naturalistic evaluation is essentially qualitative information on how people in a programme are experiencing that programme. It tries to get both feelings and facts. It asks the questions 'Why?' and 'How?' It wants to catch the whole complexity, the total picture. Typical questions in naturalistic evaluation are 'What is happening?' and 'Why?'.

Rationalistic evaluation tries to make systematic comparisons and correlations. Typical questions are 'How are women learners different from male learners in their numeracy scores?' and 'Are learners who are good in reading also good in writing?' Such questions are be best answered by evaluators outside the framework of the supervisor's visit.

It would be wonderful if each and every visit of the supervisor became a study in the naturalistic mode conducted in participation with teachers, learners and community leaders – that is, all those who hold a stake in the success of the programme.

In a very real sense, the total visit of the supervisor is evaluative. The evaluations must be shared with the appropriate stake-holders. Nobody should be kept guessing. The teacher should know what the supervisor saw and what he or she thought. The learners should know what the supervisor saw and what he or she thought of their work and performance. The community leaders should know what the supervisor saw and did and what he or she thought.

The *Training Manual for Trainers of Functional Literacy Instructors*, prepared for the National Literacy Programme in Malawi, lists the following tasks for the literacy supervisor:

- publicizing the literacy programme at local levels
- doing needs assessments
- helping to prepare relevant curricula and instructional materials
- planning and organizing training courses and recurrent meetings
- supervising literacy committees and instructors in the management of their classes
- enlisting support for the literacy programme from community leaders and extension agents
- compiling monthly reports
- distributing honoraria to instructors
- distributing functional literacy materials and equipment, and
- developing and promoting post-literacy activities.

The list provides a useful summary of items discussed in the chapter.

THINGS TO DO OR THINK ABOUT

1. How often does your supervisor visit you in the village? Does the supervisor stay overnight in the community? If not, how many hours on average does he or she spend in the community?

2. What kind of relationship do you have with your supervisor? What would you like the supervisor to do for you?

3. If you were a supervisor, how long would be your visits? What would you do during those visits. Make a detailed list.

Chapter Eleven

A Literacy Project, Programme or Campaign as a Total Literacy System

Thus far we have concentrated our discussions at the grassroots. We looked at the world of literacy work from the point of view of the workers at the grassroots level – literacy teachers, extension workers and their supervisors.

But who else is involved in literacy work? To whom does the supervisor report? Who are these specialists who make field visits? What is their role in the literacy programme? What does the total system look like?

These questions are answered in this chapter. We show what the total literacy system looks like. We show that an effective literacy system is often large both in size and scope.

There are, of course, other teachers and other supervisors working in other communities. There are organizers working at the various levels of the literacy system – from the local to the national level. And then there are specialists located in various places in the system: making plans, designing programmes, writing curricula, producing materials, training and evaluating. Sometimes international specialists would be involved.

Teachers should be interested in this chapter. It provides glimpses of the overall picture that will enable them to see their own work in a new light. It will spur further efforts as so much remains to be done. Overall understanding will not come if we concentrate only on local work and do not look at the total system.

This chapter is about the total system of literacy initiatives – projects, programmes and campaigns. But then, what have we been studying so far? Have we not discussed several parts of the total literacy systems already in the previous chapters?

Yes, we have studied several parts of total literacy systems. What we do in this chapter is provide a hill-top view of the total literacy system.

We discuss all the requirements for the successful implementation of a literacy initiative. Materials on the parts of the total system already presented in previous chapters are not repeated. Only brief references are made to the topics already discussed. Parts of the total system that have not been discussed so far will receive greater attention. Everything is put within one comprehensive perspective.

This chapter is divided into the following parts:

- Systems and subsystems; functions and actors
- An ideological subsystem
- A policy and planning subsystem
- An institutional and organizational subsystem
- A mobilizational subsystem
- A professional-support subsystem
- A programming and curriculum development subsystem
- A media and materials subsystem
- A training subsystem
- A teaching-learning subsystem
- A post-literacy subsystem
- An evaluation subsystem.

WORDS OF WISDOM AND VOICES FROM THE REAL WORLD

To understand the part, we must understand the whole. (Anonymous)

Systems and subsystems; functions and actors

A system is an orderly combination or arrangement of interdependent parts that adds up to a whole. The human body is a biological system; the human family is a social system; the school is an organizational system; the central government of any nation state is a political system; and so on. The interdependent parts of the system are often called subsystems.

Literacy projects, literacy programmes and literacy campaigns differ in size and scope. They also differ in their ideologies and their organization. But they are all systems. To be effective as literacy initiatives, they all have to have all the necessary parts, that is, they have to have all the necessary subsystems listed above.

Instead of talking about subsystems, one can talk of all the necessary functions to be performed. It is just a matter of convenience whether we use the word subsystems or functions. After all, subsystems have to perform some functions and accomplish some tasks.

One can even go further and talk of functionaries, that is, the actors in the subsystem or in the total system. Tasks and functions are, of course, performed by actors. Hence the subsystems listed above can also be seen as actors and groups of actors, performing many actions. Once again, the choice among subsystems, functions or actors is a matter of convenience. Figure 11.1 presents the total literacy system.

An ideological subsystem

The ideological subsystem is something of which literacy workers are often unaware. Or, they choose not to deal with it because it is 'political'. Politics are seen as troublesome. Therefore, nobody wants to talk about them.

The ideological subsystem is, however, impossible to neglect. Often, therefore, the ideological issues are discussed under different labels – as the philosophy of adult literacy or as values underlying the literacy programme.

THE OBJECTIVES OF THE IDEOLOGICAL SUBSYSTEM

The objective of an ideological subsystem is to give a 'soul' to the body of a literacy programme. Only by facing ideological questions can one draw strength from the cultural reservoirs of a community or nation. In one country, 'Liberation of the enslaved' may be the source of strength. In another, it may be 'Empowering of the powerless'. In one place, illiteracy may be seen as the 'Sin and Shame' of the nation; in another, literacy may be promoted as a 'Human Right'. At a more concrete level, the ideological subsystem should give everyone, from the policy-maker to the literacy teacher, a set of values to use in making choices.

We should note that the ideology of a literacy programme is not always congruent with the ideology of the nation-state. Quite often the ideology of literacy serves the purposes of change and renewal. Sometimes it may even be part of a protest movement.

Are literacy teachers far away from the ideological questions? Not at all! In fact, teachers and others at the grassroots can make ideology come to life at the field level. On the other hand, they can subvert the programme's ideology.

IMPORTANT IDEOLOGICAL ISSUES

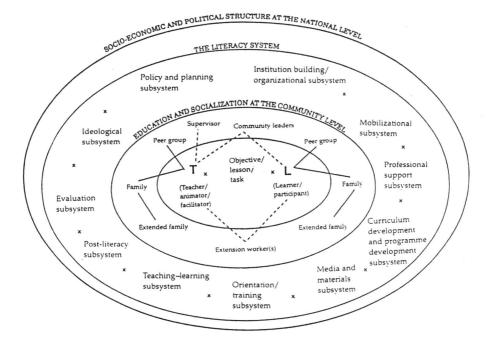

Figure 11.1 The basic teaching-learning relationship within the total social-technical system (H.S. Bhola, 1991)

The following issues have come to be important in the ideological debate on adult literacy:

1. Is international support for literacy from organizations such as UNESCO a reflection of interrelations of dominance by the West?

2. Does literacy, to be pro-people, always have to be anti-state? Can't the government ever offer a literacy programme in the interest of and on behalf of the people?

3. Should people with narrow purposes be allowed to teach literacy – for example, to professionalize labour for their factories and farms, or to convert people to particular religious beliefs?

4. What is literacy for empowering all about – individual empowerment, structural change, or both?

5. Some important issues of ideology arise in regard to women's literacy. Do women need literacy? If literacy is taught to them, what should be the content of literacy for women?

SOME POSITIONS ON THESE ISSUES AND QUESTIONS

Our answers to these questions can be suggested as follows:

Literacy in the world system. The existence of a world system is indeed a reality. We also realize that international relations today are defined less by interdependencies and more by dependencies. We do not, however, have a conspiracy theory view of the role of international organizations.

Literacy work by the state. We do not believe that literacy to be progressive has to be anti-state or that literacy work should always be conducted by organizations other than governmental organizations.

In any case, governments in the Third World cannot be bypassed. They have at least some resources. Non-governmental organizations, on the other hand, have very few resources. This is not to say that we should not continuously question the purposes and strategies of governmental literacy programmes.

The right to teach literacy. It would be wonderful if literacy were taught everywhere and to everyone for empowerment and personal fulfilment. However, in the real world there are interest groups and institutions teaching literacy for narrow interests and selfish reasons. This should be accepted because literacy ultimately wins. Whatever the objective, or whatever the setting in which it is taught, literacy adds potential to human capacities.

Literacy for empowerment. Empowerment at the individual level is necessary, but it is not enough. This is so because empowerment at the individual level may be merely a psychological 'feel good' phenomenon. If structures do not change at the same time, individual empowerment may mean nothing. Hence, literacy programmes should work towards empowerment at both the levels of individual and community. One without the other will not help much.

Literacy for all. Finally, we subscribe to the ideology of universal literacy – 'Literacy for All'. We are particularly in favour of gender equality in literacy promotion. We believe that the boy-child and the girl-child should be valued equally. We believe the both men and women should have the equal opportunity to follow their personal interests. Gender should not open only some doors and close all others.

AT THE FIELD LEVEL

What does all this mean at the grassroots level?

For one, teachers should not look for one clear ideology for their literacy programme. Irrespective of the official ideology, some will justify literacy as a human right, others as a tool of increased productivity and still others will mix different justifications for literacy.

Indeed, it is not absolutely necessary to have a clear ideology to support literacy or even to have only one ideological justification for literacy promotion. All that matters is that literacy work be permitted and promoted. Whatever the objectives of those promoting literacy, illiterates become literate. Literacy wins. Ultimately, new literates win.

If you do not have a clear ideological statement there is no reason to wait for ideological clarification or to demand ideological purity. The ideology of literacy as a human right is all we need. This is not to say that ideological positions do not matter at all. A clear ideological position provides clear directions to policy-makers and programme-developers. It clarifies means and ends, and makes choices of content and methods easier.

A policy and planning subsystem

All subsystems are important for a system to work. The policy and planning subsystem makes decisions that have far-reaching consequences.

THE OBJECTIVES OF A POLICY AND PLANNING SUBSYSTEM

The essential objective of a policy and planning system is, of course, to convert literacy ideologies into literacy policies. In turn, these policies must evolve into plans within a particular time-frame, using particular resources.

No subsystem is an island. Subsystems are all interconnected within the total literacy system. Thus, the policy subsystem is connected with development policy, formal-education policy and cultural policy. Because of these interconnections, linkages, networks and collaborations are the key words both within and without the total literacy system.

In a healthy literacy system, the policy frame is set by policy-makers. Specialists and technicians reflect the basic policies in their planning, training, materials production, teaching and evaluation. Teachers and supervisors also act within the policy frame. By providing the feedback, they influence the policy cycle.

Yet too often the policy subsystem tends to be a weak subsystem. Policies are not always clearly defined; politics take over and planning becomes merely management of crises.

Some of the most important policy and planning issues are as follows:

1. How to reconcile the local and the global in relation to needs assessments, and the centralized and the decentralized in relation to administration of programmes.

2. What should be the structure of mobilization and delivery of the literacy services – local projects, national programme, or a mass campaign?

3. What should be the policy on the language of literacy?

4. What definition of literacy or functional literacy should serve as the basis for programme development?

5. What should be the resource generation and allocation strategies?

6. What kinds of institutional mechanisms should be created to deliver literacy?

7. What should be the priorities in regard to the selection of regions and client groups? In particular, what special actions should be taken to serve the specific needs of women?

8. What should be the policy in regard to the use of South–South assistance, that is, one developing country helping another developing country?

9. What should be the policy in regard to intermediate or appropriate technology?

SOME POSITIONS ON THE ISSUES OF POLICY AND PLANNING

Local versus global, centralized versus decentralized. We think that the local versus global as well as the centralized versus decentralized are false dichotomies.

The state, of course, has to plan from the centre for the whole nation. Therefore, it can never serve the special needs of each and every community. At the same time, communities cannot pretend to plan as if the state does not exist. Development of communities has to be planned in the context of national development agendas. Development needs and learning needs developed at the centre have to be re-invented in the local setting, in local terms.

At the same time, the issue is not really centralization versus decentralization, but the distribution of power. The real issue is the autonomy and power of participants at the lower levels of the organization. This sharing of power and responsibility across the various levels of the organization is obtained through the following stages:

- *Deconcentration*, involving opening of regional and local offices so that work at the centre can be deconcentrated and shifted to regional and local offices.

- *Delegation*, involving shifting of authority to make decisions and management of programmes to regional and local offices.

- *Devolution*, resulting in full autonomy of regional or local units in all decision-making and management, while co-ordination within the system across the various levels is maintained.

Ways of overall mobilization of efforts. Policy makers must also make decisions about the overall mode of mobilization for literacy promotion. Three approaches are possible: the project approach, the programme approach and the campaign approach. Each of the approaches reflects a particular level of commitment and a particular view about the involvement of people in the literacy effort. Literacy projects appear in the form of small efforts in separate locations as, for example, workplace literacy projects and some family literacy projects. Literacy programmes are typically national in scope, but do not necessarily seek universal literacy. Public assistance may be sought but not necessarily their leadership. Literacy campaigns typically seek universal literacy and invite involvement of all the people.

Language policy. A sort of policy consensus has emerged in terms of language policies for literacy. It is accepted that, if at all possible, literacy should be taught in the mother tongue. If the mother tongue has not been committed to writing, then literacy may be taught in an eligible regional vernacular. If neither the mother-tongue nor the regional vernacular is the 'official' language of politics and economy, then a transition from the mother-tongue literacy (or from literacy in the regional vernacular) should be arranged as part of the literacy programme.

Definition of literacy or functional literacy. As we have discussed before, universal definitions of literacy are impossible. Definitions of literacy or functional literacy must be developed and accepted within each project, programme or campaign for all practical purposes. To do this is an important function of the policy and planning subsystem.

This subsystem must also develop a vision, if not plans, for promoting particular symbioses (combinations) between the print and electronic media.

Development of resources for literacy promotion. The policy and planning system should also develop public and private resources for literacy promotion. It should be kept in mind that literacy is not an item of consumption but an investment.

The nature of literacy is truly generative, that is, literacy generates positive results in all the spheres of life in which the typical new literate engages. Returns on literacy are both personal and social. Aspects of economic life, social life, political life and cultural life all improve.

In seeking to develop local community resources, care should be taken not to take from those who already have little. On the other hand, priorities in the delivery of services should be given to those who are the most disadvantaged.

Organizational and institutional issues. Settling issues of organizing and institutionalization must also be solved by the policy and planning subsystem. Organizational issues are in fact all-pervasive. Some have already been discussed in other parts of this chapter.

But there are some typical organizational issues that must be handled by policy-makers. These are: What kinds of new roles (adult literacy teacher, women's organizer, child and family care assistant, political educator) need to be created? What should be the organizational home of literacy within the existing structures of the government? What should be the division of labour between the governmental and non-governmental organizations? How to create a system for the delivery of literacy that does not control but is an enabling system?

Priorities in focus. There are never enough resources. Even when all the necessary resources are available, planning may yet demand that the programme develop in phases and stages. Policy-makers will have to decide priorities in terms of regions, constituencies, occupational and age groups, and so forth.

International and technological issues. Finally, there might be issues regarding North–South assistance, that is, development help provided by rich nations to poor nations; and South–South assistance, in other words, development assistance provided by one developing nation to another developing nation. Questions about the level of technology may also have to be decided. Do we want to emphasize electronic media or folk media? Do we want to use silk-screen printing or the latest printing presses? Do we want to use computers for management information systems or for teaching? Or do we want to stay with pencil and paper systems? Questions about the choice of technology also relate to the technology of economic production on the farm and in the factory.

AT THE FIELD LEVEL

At the field level, teachers will often find it difficult to influence these policy decisions except in very indirect ways. But understanding the nature and background of these decisions will make things easier.

An institutional and organizational subsystem

This issue has in fact been discussed above as part of the agenda of policy issues. However, at some time, organizations and institutions come into being as 'living systems.' What was once a policy issue will become an organizational and institutional issue.

It is important that all subsystems function well and make their special contributions to the total effort. The organizational and institutional subsystem is a crucial subsystem, because it is the system that delivers.

THE OBJECTIVES OF THE ORGANIZATIONAL SUBSYSTEM

The objectives of this subsystem are:

1. To establish a core structure so that the core functions of teaching functional literacy can take place. It will mean new roles and new rules setting up structures that go from the central level down to field level.

2. To establish organizational interfaces with other ministries and departments, particularly the ministry of education and the development ministries dealing with agriculture and health. Interfaces will have to be established with non-governmental organizations as well as with professional organizations such as universities.

3. To establish a system of organizations that allow people to participate in an advisory or a collaborative role.

We should note the use of the phrase core structure. The boundaries of the core, 'official' system of literacy will be too narrow to accommodate the total system of literacy as we have indicated above. (Figures 11.2, 11.3, 11.4 and 11.5 present organizational charts of literacy systems from Benin, Ethiopia, Mali and Myanmar.)

Some of the larger issues of institution building and organization are dealt with by the policy-making subsystem. However, the following tasks and issues will have to be dealt with by the 'living subsystem' of the organization:

1. Establishing institutional relationships with universities and other educational and cultural groups to obtain advisory and professional support, as well as developing organizational patterns to work with outside consultants, task forces and commissions.

2. Establishing institutional relationships with formal education for handling questions of legitimacy and equivalences between functional literacy and school programmes.

3. Creating linkages with institutions in the sectors of economy, politics and culture so that literacy skills learned by new literates can find continuous use and strength in the context of lifelong education. At the same time creating linkages between literacy work and indigenous institutions of education and culture within the larger culture.

4. Establishing an institutional infrastructure of libraries, book shops, print shops and local newsletters to make literacy sustainable.

5. Establishing new institutions for encouraging people's participation, including mass organizations, and especially women's organizations, to reflect the special interests of women in literacy.

6. Establishing patterns for organizational renewal as well as continued capacity building in all aspects of the total system of literacy.

SOME POSITIONS ON THE TASKS AND ISSUES

Systems of professional advice. Literacy systems need not and indeed cannot have everything they need within the 'official' system of a literacy project, programme or campaign. Professional support relationships must be established with other literacy initiatives at home and abroad. Universities, institutions of research and development, and the intelligentsia should be roped in to help.

Special patterns should be developed to create and use advisory committees and technical task forces to solve particular problems in the best way possible at the time.

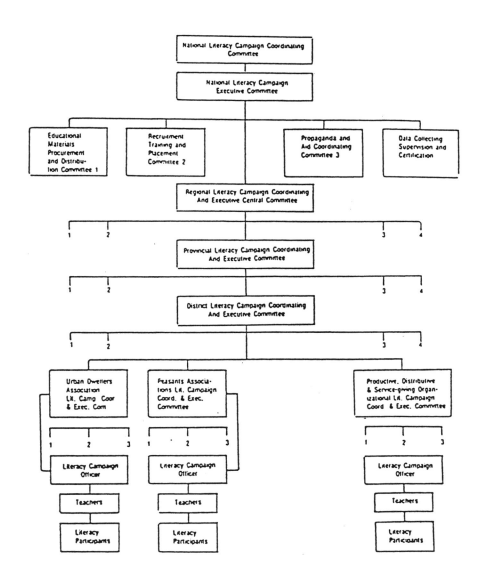

Figure 11.2 Structure of the National Literacy Compaign of Ethiopia
Source: Every Ethiopian will be Literate and Remain Literate. Addis Ababa, National Literacy Campaign Coordinating Committee. May 1981 (p.20)

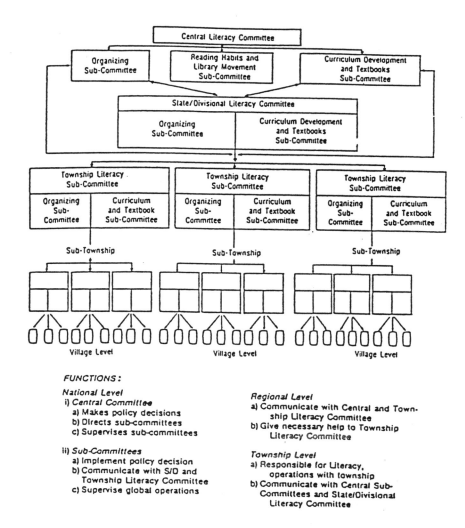

FUNCTIONS:

National Level

i) Central Committee
   a) Makes policy decisions
   b) Directs sub-committees
   c) Supervises sub-committees

ii) Sub-Committees
   a) Implement policy decision
   b) Communicate with S/D and Township Literacy Committee
   c) Supervise global operations

Regional Level
   a) Communicate with Central and Township Literacy Committee
   b) Give necessary help to Township Literacy Committee

Township Level
   a) Responsible for Literacy, operations with township
   b) Communicate with Central Sub-Committees and State/Divisional Literacy Committee

Figure 11.3 Organizational structure of literacy committees in Myanmar
Source: The National Literacy Campaign of Burma: A Case Study, in *The Struggle Against Illiteracy in Asia and the Pacific, No.3.* Bangkok, UNESCO Regional Office for Education in Asia and the Pacific, 1981 (p.35).

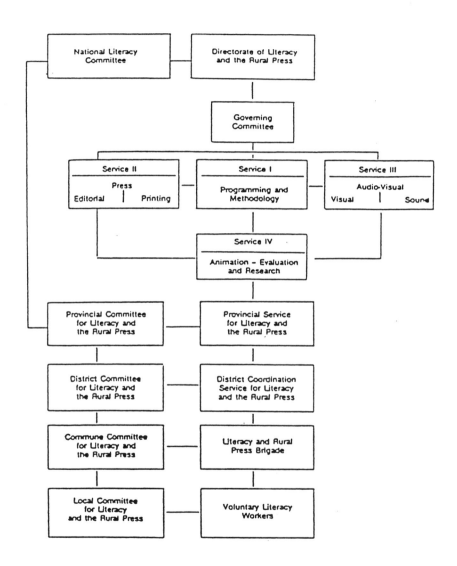

Figure 11.4 Organization of literacy work in Benin
Source: Baba Moussa (UNESCO consultant and literacy specialist)

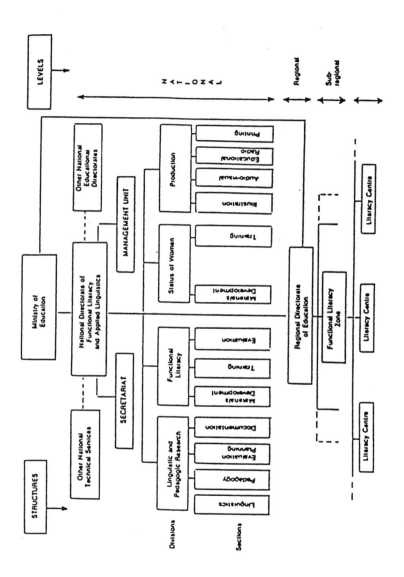

Figure 11.5 Structure of literacy operations in Mali
Source: *La direction nationale de l'alphabetisation fonctionnelle et de la linguistique appliquee - une institution malienne d'education pour la developpement,* Bamako, Ministry of Education, January 1982 (p.13).

Integrating literacy with formal education. It is unfortunate but true that the 'diploma disease' is so widespread as to have reached adult literacy classes in the farthest corners of the world. Learners in adult literacy classes want certificates.

Not only that, but too many of them seem to have the expectation that literacy will immediately result in a salaried job. Too often the economy has not yet reached the point in development to give a salaried job to the new literate. We need to break this terrible connection between literacy and a salaried job. After all, we need many more highly productive farmers and self-employed artisans, craftsmen and technicians than wage earners.

In the meantime, we need to permit adults and even more so youth to move freely between the formal school and functional adult literacy programmes. That means that adult literacy classes have to achieve levels of teaching and learning as good as or better than comparable levels in the school system. That will give adult literacy legitimacy. At the same time, specific equivalences between learning within the two systems have to be established so that those who wish to move into the formal system can do so.

Linkages with development institutions. Literacy systems must at the same time develop linkages with development institutions such as agriculture, health and labour. Extension workers in these institutions have already discovered the limits of their work with illiterate farmers and workers; they have learned that they cannot do much extension work with those who are illiterate.

There is an opportunity to develop functional literacy programmes with development institutions where the extension ministries and departments take the prior role in teaching functional literacy.

At the same time, connections should be established between the literacy system and the economic, social, political and cultural institutions. These institutions should become friendly to the new literate. The new literate should be taught the habits of making use of literacy in their interactions with these institutions.

Institutions of a literate environment. Institutions that create a literate environment and thereby sustain literacy among new literates should be established. These include rural and urban libraries, book shops that sell or rent books, print shops, newsletters, news sheets, and so forth. On the other hand, connections should be made between the literacy system and indigenous institutions of education and culture.

Institutions of people's participation. It is most important to establish some structures that provide opportunities for people's participation.

In the organizational charts for some literacy systems (see Figures 11.2 to 11.5) one can see how parallel systems for peoples' participation were developed to advise the administrative system. In Ethiopia, mass organizations of women and youth, the urban dwellers associations and the nationwide peasants' associations were put to good use. Institutional renewal and capacity building. Finally, the literacy system must look at itself every now and then, and go through systematic renewal. As part of this renewal, it is necessary continuously to build the professional capacity of individuals working within the literacy system in all aspects of literacy work.

AT THE FIELD LEVEl

Once again, even though the questions of institution building and organization are shaped by the 'Big Boys' in upper levels of the administration, teachers can influence and create special immediate environments in the communities where they work. Teachers can also make important use of the so-called indigenous institutions which are available within the communities.

A mobilizational subsystem

Motivations are not spontaneous. A mobilizational subsystem is necessary but is often neglected. Too often mobilization is seen as something done at the outset of a programme and then forgotten.

THE OBJECTIVES OF THE SUBSYSTEM OF MOBILIZATION

The objectives of a subsystem of mobilization are:

1. To get the maximum involvement of all the people to make a literacy programme a mass movement.

2. To create enthusiasm and a sense of urgency about universalizing literacy within a country or community.

3. To enable people to make personal commitments so that teachers can teach, learners can learn and communities can commit resources in cash and kind.

4. To develop thereby an environment of hope toward creating a culture of print in which all the people are participants and are engaged in a process of lifelong learning in a learning society.

Successful mobilizations enable people to take over. Literacy work becomes a mass movement. Unfortunately, not all political leaders want this to happen. Hence mobilization is neglected; narrow state control is preferred.

ISSUES IN MOBILIZATION FOR LITERACY

The mobilization issues arise from the need to balance certain elements: purposes of the state and interests of the people, education and indoctrination and persuasion and coercion.

SOME POSITIONS ON THESE ISSUES AND QUESTIONS

In whose interest? The basic question is: Whose purposes will be served through the mobilization effort – is the mobilization meant to serve the state or the people's interests, or both? Related to it is the question of control. If the state apparatus is the only instrument of mobilization and if the people themselves are not involved, then there may be a problem.

Education versus indoctrination. The second issue can be seen to lie between education and indoctrination. Successful mobilization involves passion and emotion. But good mobilization is education made passionate. Mobilization based only on emotion is likely to be manipulative.

Persuasion versus coercion. The third issue in mobilization is about persuasion versus coercion. Communicating to persuade is acceptable. Persistence in trying to persuade is acceptable as well, if it is within reasonable limits. But imposing on people and violating their privacy is not acceptable. Threat and coercion are completely out of the question.

The state can engage in structural mobilization as well. That is, the state can sometimes create a set of incentives and disincentives to encourage the public to take a certain course and not another. In the choice of incentives and disincentives, there should be choice. Those who do not make the 'right' choice should not be unduly punished.

Mobilization on behalf of women. Mobilization of women and mobilization in behalf of women should be paid special attention in literacy work. Often, men insist on keeping their wives and daughters home for domestic work and do not want them to attend literacy classes to put those 'new-fangled ideas' in their heads.

AT THE FIELD LEVEL

At the field level, the teacher finds him- or herself engaged in continuous mobilization, face-to-face with participants, non-participants and leaders in the community. Of course, the teacher as well as all other field workers should protect the educational and moral tenor of their efforts of mobilization.

Workers at the grassroots should pay special attention to the use of the oral and the indigenous media to promote literacy. Songs, skits and rural drama quickly come to mind as examples.

A professional support subsystem

For decades literacy programmes lived off the crumbs from the table of formal education. Too often children's primers were given to adults to read. They were expected to find them interesting!

Even today, literacy programmes are seen in a most narrow perspective as a matter of a teacher, a group of adults, a primer and a chalkboard. It is only recently that we have started talking about literacy projects, programmes and campaigns as systems of delivery and as systems of professional work.

We know today that professional 'knowledge' is needed for all the various subsystems of the total literacy system. Theory and research are necessary for policy and planning, institution building, mobilization, curriculum development, teaching, training, and evaluation.

Professional 'support' is needed clearly and directly for providing training of personnel and for research support in regard to needs assessment and curriculum development, study of languages, vocabularies, methods of teaching, materials design, testing and evaluation.

THE OBJECTIVES OF THE PROFESSIONAL SUPPORT SUBSYSTEM

The objectives of the professional support subsystem are clearly the following:

1. To obtain or create the knowledge base of theory and research for systematic Research–Development–Diffusion process necessary for effective literacy programmes in all aspects of planning, programming, curriculum development, implementation, training, teaching and evaluation.

2. Through systematic reflection and evaluation to consolidate the experience of doing literacy work to be able to share with others the experiences and the insights that could be used in future work.

ISSUES IN PROFESSIONAL SUPPORT

A few of the important issues in professional support of adult literacy work are as follows:

1. International influences on the ideology and the technology of adult literacy around the world.

2. Distribution of labour between the 'official' system of literacy (i.e., literacy project, programme or campaign) and the infrastructure of research and development in the larger society in providing professional support to adult literacy initiatives.

3. The theory and practice gap within the producers of knowledge on the one hand and within the groups of practitioners on the other hand.

4. Should an adult educator first be politically committed and then be an expert? Or should it be the other way around?

5. Production of knowledge that reflects the realities of the disadvantaged and serves their interests, especially in regard to women.

SOME POSITIONS ON THE ISSUES AND QUESTIONS

Knowledge in the world system. The professional support issues have an international colour as well. While literacy is a person-to-person encounter of learning to read, ideally in the mother-tongue and within highly localized settings, a lot of encouragement to adult literacy has come from international sources, foremost among them UNESCO. It is hard to imagine what the current status of adult literacy might be worldwide if UNESCO had not led the literacy movement since its inception. Most of the basic and policy research in adult education and adult literacy has come from international organizations such as the UNESCO Institute for Education (UIE), the International Bureau of Education (IBE) and the International Council for Adult Education (ICAE).

Ironically, 98 per cent of the world's illiterate people live in the Third World but the most important initiatives in theory, research and training have been taken in Western universities. Universities in Africa and Asia have started initiatives in this regard, but more needs to be done. In the meantime, literacy programmes in the Third World need to establish South–South exchanges of technical assistance whereby one Third World country assists another. They also need to learn to adapt research from the West and from international sources to their own local conditions.

The need for professional networks. There is the need to establish a division of labour between the 'official' system of adult literacy and the research and development infrastructure in universities and specialized research institutions. The 'official' subsystem of professional support within a literacy programme will never be able to provide all the professional support needed by the system by itself. The official system could carry out vocabulary research for writing primers and follow up books. It could do needs assessment at the local level. It could do applied research in teaching–learning, and training of lower level personnel. Almost everything else by way of basic and policy research has to come from the outside.

Bringing theory and practice together. The theory–practice gap appears in at least two ways. On the one hand, university researchers do not to have much by way of practical field experience. On the other hand, field workers lack theoretical knowledge and are unable to analyse and consolidate their own experiences. Things need fixing at both ends.

Professionalism or gradualism? There is also the issue of professionalism versus gradualism. This issue was expressed forcefully by Mao Zedong in the form of 'red versus expert'. Does an adult educator or adult literacy worker have to be ideologically committed (that is, be 'Red') or does he or she have to be an expert? In Mao's China, the 'Red' won over the 'Expert'. Adult educators elsewhere are also worried that with too much emphasis on professionalization, we may be formalizing adult education so much as to make it impossible for the 'uncredentialled but educated' to do adult literacy work. We need well-trained people to do adult education work. The right to serve and the right to teach must be protected for all citizens who want to join in literacy work!

Knowledge to reflect total reality. Finally, it must be assured that knowledge produced does reflect the realities of the poor and the disadvantaged, particularly the lives of poor women around the world. More and more women must be associated as full members of the institutions of knowledge production. The same must be done in regard to minorities.

AT THE FIELD LEVEL

At the field level, adult literacy programmes should do at least two things: create practical knowledge within a national plan and create local knowledge at the local levels.

The system of resource centres established by the literacy programme in India is a good example. The Directorate of Adult Education and the National Institute of Adult Education serve as a national resource centre. This is followed by a network of state resource centres. Some districts have district resource units. There is a division of labour among these centres placed at the various levels, each providing the services of literacy promotion that it is best equipped and best located to provide.

Nothing can substitute for the local knowledge obtained from the action and reflection of individual teachers and other grassroots workers. This knowledge will need to be validated through participatory work with learners.

A programming and curriculum development subsystem

This is an important subsystem because it chooses what is taught and determines the context of the teaching-learning process.

THE OBJECTIVES OF THE PROGRAMMING AND CURRICULUM DEVELOPMENT SUBSYSTEM

The objectives of this subsystem are as follows:

1. To choose the Knowledge-Attitude-Performance components and levels of a particular functional literacy programme.

2. To choose the general strategies of integration between literacy and functionality, and literacy and awareness.

3. To choose context, structure and patterns of delivery of the curriculum, that is: Who will teach? What? Where? When? and In what long-term time-frame? With what expected effects?

This is one of those subsystems that must be planned within the boundaries of the official literacy system. The actual implementation of the curriculum, however, involves many actors and institutions outside the boundaries of the official system.

ISSUES IN CURRICULUM AND PROGRAMME DEVELOPMENT

The following issues are important:

1. What will be the language of literacy, and how and when to transfer from the mother tongue to the national or official language of literacy? (This is also an issue for the policy and planning subsystem.)

2. What would be the focus of functionality? Should a non-economic focus be considered as functional? What should be the knowledge content of functionality rooted in awareness?

3. If a beginning is made with focus on the objective of economic functionality, how could objectives be made more general later? Must the teaching of economic functionality always include a component of income-generating activities?

4. What should be the method of integration? What level of integration should be achieved?

5. How to ensure that the curriculum and the programme does not simply reinforce traditional roles that domesticate women.

6. How to relate to pre-literacy and post-literacy programmes?

7. How is the curriculum of the project or programme related to formal education?

You may want to look back at Chapter 4 on curriculum and programme development. Most of these issues have already been discussed in that chapter in detail. It will be repetitious to include a discussion of the same issues in this space. Readers are invited to review the earlier material on these topics.

AT THE FIELD LEVEL

Teachers have an important part to play. They bring curriculum alive in the lives of learners; they make the programme generative, bringing changes to the lives of people beyond the classroom. They won't be able to do this unless they are encouraged and assisted.

In spite of all the talk about serving the special interests of women and minorities, this rarely happens in the field. Teachers need to become more sensitive to women's issues. For example, women's programmes continue to be focused on domestic work. In some countries in West Africa, women produce and sell food, but they are denied the credit they need. Women in income-generating activities have often ended up with more work and no rewards leading to greater oppression.

A media and materials subsystem

The media and materials subsystem is, again, an important subsystem. Ideology, policy, curriculum and methodology all become concrete in media and materials.

THE OBJECTIVES OF THE MEDIA AND MATERIALS SUBSYSTEM

This subsystem aims to procure from outside or to produce within the system materials of all kinds for functional literacy programmes and for teachers, learners and other facilitators for the pre-literacy, literacy and post-literacy stages of literacy work. Thus, nine different needs of teaching-learning materials have to be fulfilled (see Figure 11.6).

	pre-literacy stage	literacy stage	Post-literacy stage
Learners' materials	1	2	3
Teachers' materials	4	5	6
Other materials	7	8	9

Figure 11.6 A teaching/learning materials guide

Media and materials subsystems neither can nor should try to produce everything within the subsystem.

ISSUES IN THE CONTEXT OF MEDIA AND MATERIALS

Here are some of the relevant issues:

1. Can folk media and electronic media be used to promote print media, that is, literacy?

2. Is the production of local materials really feasible?

3. How do you write and publish follow-up materials for new readers in newly literate cultures?

4. Are women equally and justly reflected in the materials produced?

SOME POSITIONS ON THE ISSUES AND QUESTIONS

Once, again, media and materials have been discussed in detail earlier in this *Sourcebook*. Here we will comment on some of the issues that merit further attention.

Media access is not universal. Specialists within this subsystem need to be aware that access to radio and television is not as widespread to the disadvantaged as once thought. In spite of the so-called transistor revolution, radio has not become available to the poor. Television is often out of the question. Wherever these media have become available, they do not necessarily broadcast educational programmes.

Possibilities with radio. That does not mean that nothing can be done by literacy workers. The media and materials subsystems must work with the media of newspapers, radio and television to support the literacy effort of the country.

Radio stations can be used for several purposes, among them: to mobilize learners and teachers and community leaders; to broadcast information dealing with functionality and awareness components of the literacy programme; and to promote continuous in-service teacher training.

Local newspapers. Newspapers could be persuaded to issue one special page a day or a week, as appropriate, for new literates. Special newspapers for new literates have been tried with considerable success in several countries such as the United Republic of Tanzania and Mali.

Writers' workshops. My experience with writers' workshops have been quite positive. Writers' workshops can be used to produce relevant need-based primers as well as follow-up reading materials. Literacy teachers and supervisors, extension workers and even literacy learners themselves can join such workshops.

Sharing primers. Literacy primers are generally produced within the literacy system. This need not always be so. If cultural, social and economic conditions are similar, there is no reason for each project or each region to have different primers. Smaller literacy systems should look around. Wherever possible, they should conserve their resources and use primers already available.

Follow-up books; co-operating with development ministries. Writers' workshops have been used successfully to develop follow-up reading materials for the newly literate. It is possible for literacy systems to collaborate with other development ministries to produce such materials. Everywhere in the world, government ministries and departments write and publish development materials on the subjects of agriculture, health, family planning, labour laws, and so forth. Unfortunately, almost everywhere these materials are written in difficult-to-read language. Sometimes the language of the materials is not the language of literacy. These should be adapted to the levels of new readers.

Publication channels for literacy materials. Publishing special materials for new literates is not a profit-making business. Private publishers seldom publish books for new literates. As a result special channels for the production of materials for new literates must be created. It is not necessary for each literacy system to have its own follow-up books.

Follow-up books should definitely be shared among different literacy systems as widely as possible.

Paper famine; necessity of multiple uses. One must also keep in mind the reality of an acute paper famine in the developing world. We must think of 'multiple uses' of the same materials through rural libraries and reading rooms. These materials should be brought to the attention of the widest possible reading public in the community.

AT THE FIELD LEVEL

At this level, the best teachers and other grassroots workers can do is to use folk and indigenous media for both motivation and instruction. Another most important idea to follow is co-operation with rural newspapers involving teachers and learners working together to collect, write and read news.

A training subsystem

The training subsystem is a crucial subsystem because it builds capacity within the total system. Literacy programmes often create new roles in new contexts. People have to be prepared for these new roles and others already within the system have to learn to deal with new roles.

The objective of the training subsystem is essentially to orient, train, socialize and upgrade all role incumbents within a literacy system. Once again we can not do everything within the literacy system – universities and other specialized institutions will have to help.

ISSUES IN LITERACY TRAINING

Training issues can relate to the whole system and can include the training of trainers, organizers and even policy makers. There are three different processes: orientation of high officials and leaders; formal training of functionaries; and socialization through which new values and new habits of thought, talk and action are taught. Training can be pre-service and in-service.

The discussion below focuses on the core issues of training the grassroots worker – the literacy teacher. Some of the special issues concerned are as follows:

1. Should we recruit school leavers, primary-school teachers and/or retired army personnel or should we expect extension workers to teach functional literacy? What other recruitment pools for recruiting literacy teachers are available?

2. Should we have part-time teachers or full-time literacy teachers?

3. What kinds of training schemes should be designed for teachers who are volunteers, part-time and have a quick turnover?

4. Should the role of a literacy teacher be confined to the teaching of reading, writing and numeracy or should the teacher be expected to teach functional knowledge as well? How should the teacher be trained to teach functional knowledge?

5. Should the teacher also be trained as a development agent?

6. Should the teacher be given technical training only or ideological training as well?

7. Should the community select the teacher or should the project select the teachers they would train and employ?

8. How to ensure that women get the right representation within projects and programmes as teacher trainers and as teacher trainees. How to ensure that other minorities, refugees and tribesmen/ tribeswomen also get suitable representation.

SOME POSITIONS ON THESE TRAINING ISSUES AND QUESTIONS

Since we have discussed the role and function of the literacy teacher several times in the *Sourcebook*, many of the issues are not new.

Full-time literacy teachers unlikely. Unless adult education becomes institutionalized as in China, no system could conceivably afford a full-time adult educator or an adult literacy worker. They will not have a full-day's work awaiting them. It is most likely that adult literacy work for a long time will remain part-time. Again, the current level of funding for adult education being what it is, adult literacy work will also remain voluntary.

Need for substantial training inputs. Even though adult literacy teachers are part-time and will continue to have a quick turnover, the maximum possible training inputs should be made. When they are attracted to other jobs or leave their jobs to engage in personal income-generating activities, it should not be considered a loss to the project but a mark of success of their adult education.

Teaching literacy; managing functionality and awareness. The adult literacy teacher should be seen at the core as the teacher of literacy skills, but at the same time must be seen as the manager of all aspects of a functional literacy programme. He or she should be the nerve centre of functional literacy work in the community. Literacy ideology and technology should be given due attention, as should women functionaries, women learners and content of teaching and training.

The best a teacher of adult literacy can do at the field level in terms of training is to take responsibility for his or her own self-training and continuous growth. This will come through reading, through reflection on his or her own daily work, and from the opportunity of discussing ideas and problems with other teachers in the community or in the vicinity.

A teaching–learning subsystem

The teaching–learning subsystem is the heart of the matter. Objectives are to deliver literacy instruction, integrated with functionality and awareness, generalizable to become lifelong education. The boundaries of the subsystem are not the class but the community.

ISSUES IN THE TEACHING–LEARNING SUBSYSTEM

The following are some of the important issues within this subsystem:

1. Can the adult literacy teacher, a typical school leaver volunteering to work for a small honorarium, handle all we expect from him or her – literacy, functionality and awareness?

2. Is it possible for a typical adult literacy teacher to acquire the competence in subject matter and the human sensibilities that we expect?

3. Is true integration in the content of literacy, functionality and awareness even possible?

4. How are women treated in mixed classes?

SOME POSITIONS ON THESE ISSUES AND QUESTIONS

This author is of the view that none of the ideas discussed in this *Sourcebook* are beyond the reach of adult literacy teachers whether they work in New York or in a village in Senegal. Literacy teachers can be trained to teach literacy, functionality and awareness, if properly assisted. They can be made aware of the special needs of particular groups such as women and ethnic minorities. What is needed the right combination of political commitment and professional competence.

AT THE FIELD LEVEL

The teacher is the most important actor within this subsystem. He or she is the person in direct personal contact with learners and community leaders. We have talked of the need for the teacher to be committed and competent. We invite the teacher to respond.

A post-literacy subsystem

This subsystem, like some of the other subsystems, is very important but often neglected. Some literacy workers go as far to say that it is useless to do literacy work if post-literacy work can not be planned before literacy. We would not go that far. If it is not possible to plan post-literacy work that does not mean that literacy work should not be done! After all, literacy can be made sustainable if taught well the first time around. Those who lose some of their skills will re-learn them much more easily and quickly. Even those who learned only rudimentary literacy skills would have been introduced to the culture of print.

THE OBJECTIVES OF THE POST-LITERACY SUBSYSTEM

The objectives of the post-literacy subsystem are the following:

1. To encourage and assist newly literate adults to continue reading and writing, thereby making literacy sustainable.

2. To provide some formal structures such as the 'study circle' as a forum for new literate adults and others to come together to discuss what they have read and make decisions about community development.

3. To expand the conception of communication within literacy and post-literacy systems to include all media – folk media, print media and electronic media – and help adults develop their own individual media mix for information handling.

4. To help establish centres in which new literate adults learn to make use of their literacy in their social, economic, political and cultural lives.

5. To help establish structures and infrastructures of the print culture – newsletters, libraries, bookshop, etc. – to support the reading habit and use of print in all aspects of life.

6. Thereby connecting newly literate adults and all other readers in the community with the new learning society engaged in lifelong education for all.

The post-literacy subsystem is not confined to the 'official' system of literacy. It has wide boundaries that encompass the total community and media institutions both local and national.

POST-LITERACY ISSUES

1. Is it possible even to conceptualize a learning society and lifelong education without an expanding economy and a vibrant culture?

2. What comes first, a literate environment or post-literacy work and institutions of a literate society?

3. How do we get out of the old conception of post-literacy work as merely publishing follow-up materials to help people to retain their literacy skills?

4. How do we promote actual uses of literacy in the economic, social and political sectors?

5. How do we reconcile the realities of the paper famine and costs of publication of books with the universal need to read?

6. How do we relate post-literacy work with formal education systems to assist those who want a second chance within the formal system, without making post-literacy work a mere surrogate of formal schooling?

7. How do we ensure that the effects of literacy on individuals, within families, across genders, and classes are functional and not regressive or exploitative?

SOME POSITIONS ON THESE ISSUES AND QUESTIONS

What comes first? Is post-literacy work possible without an expanding economy and a vibrant culture? The question should in fact be reformulated like this: Is an expanding future economy and a vibrant culture in the future possible without putting the present economy and culture in a give-and-take relationship with post-literacy work and institutions? The answer is 'No'.

Of course, there are no 'firsts' and 'seconds' in social change. Post-literacy work cannot wait for an expanding economy and a vibrant culture to come first. Indeed, post-literacy work and institutions have to be both an instrument and a product of an expanding economy and a vibrant culture.

Post-literacy work and a literate environment. The same mutual relationship exists between post-literacy work and a literate environment. We do not wait for the literate environment to come first and then do literacy or post-literacy work. By doing literacy and post-literacy work we create a literate environment.

More than a matter of literacy retention. For too long, we have conceptualized post-literacy work as merely writing and publishing follow-up materials to save new literates from relapse into illiteracy. We need to expand the concept of post-literacy work along its various dimensions. On the one hand, it should be more than print. It should include a mix from all media as the new literate engages in the new role of information gathering and use. At the same time, the concept should be expanded from merely skills acquisition to use in knowledge acquisition, in problem solving and in social action.

Promoting uses of literacy. Promoting actual uses of literacy in the economic, social and political aspects of an individual's life will not be easy. But situations must be created wherein newly literate adults can be assisted in using literacy skills for personal effectiveness.

Multiple uses of materials. The paper famine prevailing in most of the Third World is real. The costs of publication and, therefore, of buying books and magazines are high. These facts fly in the face of the universal need to read. How are the African adults in rural areas going to afford to buy a book if it costs them a fortune? We must invent patterns (rural libraries, reading clubs, etc.) to promote multiple uses of materials whereby the same book can be read by a number of people.

Post-literacy work and formal education. Post-literacy work has to be interfaced with the formal education system if that is what the people want. We must assist those who want a second chance within the formal system. But the overall integrity of post-literacy work must be protected. It must not be allowed to become a mere surrogate of formal schooling.

New exploitations of literacy and symbolic capital. Considerable vigilance will be required to see that the new reality of literacy within individuals, within families, across genders, and classes is functional and not exploitative. The new literate individual should not be allowed to develop a mix among media wherein print plays no part. Within families, all should be encouraged to learn to read – special care must be taken to see that the mother and the girl child are not disadvantaged.

In terms of social classes, it should be ensured that literates do not establish new landlordism of symbolic capital whereby they use their own literacy skills to lead and manage projects while the illiterate sweat for them on farms and in craft sheds.

AT THE FIELD LEVEL

Within limits, the adult literacy teacher can help promote post-literacy initiatives. If one community in which the teacher teaches becomes a literate community with a literate environment, it is an occasion for satisfaction and pride.

An evaluation subsystem

This is an important subsystem. Everyone wants it for accountability and for effectiveness.

The objective of an evaluation subsystem is to make a programme system, a healthy culture of information that creates and uses descriptive as well as evaluative information.

The boundaries of an evaluation subsystem are not narrow. They should be broad enough to include national universities and literacy organizations abroad.

ISSUES IN THE EVALUATION SUBSYSTEM

1. The first issue is implied in the two categories of information.

2. Evaluation is, of course, also caught in a philosophic discussion of how it should be conducted – the so-called debate on the para-digm shift from the positivist to the naturalistic.

3. Descriptive data versus evaluative data is another issue.

4. External evaluation conducted by outsiders versus internal evalu-ation conducted by insiders is another.

5. Should literacy evaluation cover only literacy skills or should it also test for achievement and progress in all the three components?

6. What should be the criteria for the study of impact and the need to study impact on the lives of women.

ACTORS IN THE EVALUATION SUBSYSTEM

Too often literacy workers look at evaluation as something done by evaluation specialists coming from the outside. But that is not the whole story.

Evaluation done by the evaluation specialist is important, but it is only a part of the complete evaluation subsystem. Typically, evaluation specialists organize Management Information Systems (MISs), work out comparisons and correlations, and conduct impact evaluations. That is, they determine the impact of the functional literacy programme on the lives of participants and their communities.

More than half of the evaluation burden is carried by people other than the evaluation specialists. The evaluation subsystem includes the policy-makers at the top, and the literacy teacher and the learners at the grassroots. More than half the time, there is no separation between the decision-maker and the evaluator, between the teacher and the evaluator, and between the learner and the evaluator.

LEARNERS AS EVALUATORS

Learners are part of the evaluator subsystem because they will be engaged in self-evaluations. They will also be involved, as equal partners, in participatory evaluations conducted in collaboration with teachers, supervisors and community leaders.

TEACHERS AS EVALUATORS

Teachers, of course, are important actors within the evaluation subsystem. They keep attendance registers to record the functioning of the class. How many learners are enrolled? How many are men? How many are women? How many are regular and how many are not so regular? How many dropped out and when? Looking over these figures from month to month, the teacher can determine the progress of the class in terms of numbers.

The teacher also administers some ready-made tests of reading, writing and functional knowledge, thereby keeping a record of rates of learning and of achievement of learners.

The teacher also writes a daily journal. This journal typically includes qualitative remarks on the conduct of the class such as the present morale of learners and their level of motivation. The journal also includes information about what learners are doing with their newly acquired literacy skills. Breakdowns and failures will also be recorded so that help can be received from the supervisor on improving things.

SUPERVISOR AS EVALUATOR

The supervisor's role in evaluation is very important indeed. It is at the level of the supervisor that a third-person evaluation perspective emerges.

The supervisor consolidates all data received from thirty to fifty teachers under the supervisor's charge. By comparing, the supervisor can note whether problems of attendance and dropout are general or specific to certain communities. By consolidating, the supervisor gets the complete picture.

The supervisor also develops a qualitative picture of the programme in his or her area from the various journal entries received from the teachers. To all this, the supervisor adds his or her own observations and perceptions. This is then sent to the next level of the literacy programme management.

EVALUATION BY PROGRAMME SPECIALISTS

Most programme specialists, and especially curriculum developers, materials writers and producers, and trainers have to conduct their own evaluations in order to judge the effectiveness of their inputs.

They conduct two types of evaluations: formative evaluation and summative evaluation. Formative evaluation is evaluation conducted during the formation (that is, the development and preparation) of plans, curricula and materials. Summative evaluation is done to sum up the results.

Curriculum evaluation. Curriculum evaluation starts with needs assessment. It then seeks to determine whether the curriculum actually met the needs as assessed. It also asks questions about choices of curricular activities included in the curriculum to teach functional literacy. Were the choices right? Were the contents and levels of knowledge, skills and attitudes appropriate? There can be several other questions.

Materials evaluation. This is also called product evaluation. Individual items of instructional materials are evaluated to see if the product fulfils the objectives that were intended to be achieved?

Training evaluation. In training evaluation, the effectiveness of training content, process and effect are evaluated. Is the training preparing people for the roles they will play in the field? Does it actually improve performance? Does it make trainees problem-solvers? Could training be made more efficient and more effective?

EVALUATION BY EVALUATION SPECIALISTS

Evaluation tasks described above do not exhaust all the evaluation needs of an effective literacy system. There are important evaluation tasks that must be performed by evaluation specialists.

Evaluation specialists working on a literacy project are full-time evaluators and their concerns are generally with impact evaluation.

THE ESSENTIAL EVALUATION AGENDA

1. To be able to describe the status of a programme at a particular time.

2. To be able to choose between various ends of a programme or to validate ends as established.

3. To be able to choose between various means to achieve chosen ends.

4. To be able to measure the impact of the programme on the lives of individuals and their communities.

THE NECESSARY INFORMATION

The evaluation subsystem must think of 'information above evaluation', that is, information being the real concern rather than evaluation.

Information should be seen in two parts: descriptive information and evaluative information broken down into information obtained through naturalistic evaluation, and information obtained through rationalistic evaluation.

Tools and instruments of descriptive information, for example, are class registers, journals, instructor's and supervisor's reports (see for example Figure 11.7), results of tests in reading and writing administered to learners in classes, recruitment and educational data on teachers, teacher tests during training, and so on. Tabulations, graphs and descriptive statistics are also used. Questions relate to size and scope, and to quantitative changes in the size and scope.

Tools and techniques of naturalistic evaluation are qualitative. The evaluator himself or herself is the instrument. Conversations with all possible stakeholders are recorded. Themes are discovered and reports are written as case-studies. Questions are answered about the experience of participants with the programme and the impact they see on their lives and on life surrounding them.

Tools and techniques of rationalistic evaluation are formal and pre-tested instruments such as structured interviews, tests and structured observations. Data processing is typically statistical in nature. Questions answered are about comparisons and correlations.

FUNCTIONAL LITERACY PROGRAMME

Monthly Report
(To be completed by Instructor and submitted to Supervisor)

1. At the end of the month of: _____ Year: _____

2. Village _____

3. Name of Instructor: _____

4. Group name _____

5. Number of learners at the end of the month: Male: ___Female:____

6. Total number of lessons held per month: _____

7. Number of learners who absented the whole month:
   Male: ___Female:____

8. Number of learners who discontinued: Male:___Female:____

9. Average monthly attendance _____

10. Equipment required _____

11. Number of days supervisor visited class _____

12. Number of days extension agents visited class _____

     (a) Agriculture extension agent _____
     (b) Health extension agent   _____
     (c) Home economics worker   _____
     (d) Others (name)

13. Last lesson taught at the end of the month: _____

14. What was done to reduce learner drop-out? What was done to bring back
    drop-outs to the class? _____

15. Comments: _____

16. When was the last Honoraria paid: _____

17. Literacy Committee Chairman's comments: _____

18. Chairman's Signature:_____ Date: _____

19. Instructors Signature:_____ Date: _____

Figure 11.7 Examples of monthly report forms from Malawi.
Source: Malawi M15

FUNCTIONAL LITERACY PROGRAMME

<u>Monthly Report II</u> by Supervisor
(To be filled by the Supervisor and sent to the Project Officer)

Month ending:_____   Year: _____

Name of Supervisor:_____   Name of E.P.A.: _____

1. Number of instructors/instructresses at the end of the month:
                                 Male:_____ Female:_____

2. Instructors/instructresses who dropped out during the month

Name of instructor/instructress	Reasons

3. Classes which discontinued during the month

Name of class	M	F	MF	Reasons

4. Report on Attendance
   Comments: Action taken: Proposals for remedial action:

5. Materials needed (please specify): _____
_____
_____

6. Instructors received Honorarium up to the month of: _____
   Comments: _____
_____

7. Any other comments: _____
_____

Date: _____   Signature of Supervisor: _____

The ultimate objective of the evaluation sub-culture is to create 'a culture of information' within the literacy system – a way of doing things at work which involves information collection, information sharing and information use to make good decisions.

The most important themes in adult literacy evaluation today are: (1) evaluation of learner achievement, (2) continuous monitoring of programmes and (3) evaluation of the impact of the programme.

The most important philosophic step in learner achievement is that the learner take part in his or her own evaluation of achievement. Such a step has already been taken by the ETS Tests of Applied Literacy Skills developed in the United States that use a set of three tests as follows:

- The prose literacy test measures the skills and knowledge needed to read and interpret materials such as newspaper articles, magazines and books.

- The document literacy test measures the skills and knowledge needed to identify and use information located in materials such as charts, forms, tables and indexes.

- The quantitative literacy test measures the skills and knowledge needed to apply arithmetic operations to information contained in printed materials such as a loan or sale advertisement and order form or a checkbook.

Learner achievement includes more than these three tests. Individual learner's 'profile sheets' (sheets of paper showing actual practice of literacy in real life) are used to get snapshots of literacy proficiencies. Thus testing works with a mix of standardized testing, materials-based testing, competency-based testing and participatory assessment.

The participatory part of evaluation allows informal testing that permits personal perspectives. Curriculum established by programme specialists is thus integrated with goals and needs identified by adults themselves.

Programme monitoring is typically focused in management information systems (MISs). These can be simple pencil-and paper systems using data generated by a programme in the course of its implementation. At times it could be nothing more than half a dozen tables and charts, completed each month, on the basis of an attendance register, test results from classes, and interviews with learners and community leaders.

<hr>

IMPACT EVALUATION

Impact evaluation can be handled in various ways and at various levels. At the national and regional levels, it will generally be handled by teams of trained evaluators. They may use both rationalistic and naturalistic approaches.

At the community and classroom levels, impact can be studied by a sensitive teacher or a grassroots worker on his or her own. It will be best done as participative evaluation. A group may sit down together and ask themselves questions What have we learned from this literacy programme? How is the programme affecting our lives and the lives of those around us?

THINGS TO DO OR THINK ABOUT

In this chapter, we have dealt with the eleven subsystems listed below. Now think about your own literacy system in which you are working. How well do you think the various subsystems are functioning. For 'Very well' circle 5; for 'Just adequate' circle 3; and for 'Much room for improvement' circle 1.

An ideological subsystem	5 3 1
A policy and planning subsystem	5 3 1
An institutional and organizational subsystem	5 3 1
A mobilizational subsystem	5 3 1
A professional-support subsystem	5 3 1
A programming and curriculum development subsystem	5 3 1
A media and materials subsystem	5 3 1
A training subsystem	5 3 1
A teaching–learning subsystem	5 3 1
A post-literacy subsystem	5 3 1
An evaluation subsystem	5 3 1

Chapter Twelve

Conclusions

This is the concluding chapter of the book. You may want to review the table of contents to see just what this *Sourcebook* has covered.

> Education makes a people easy to lead, but difficult to drive; easy to govern but impossible to enslave. (Lord Brougham)

> What would happen, if the whole world would become literate? Answer: not very much, for the world is by and large structured in such a way that it is capable of absorbing the impact. But if the whole world consisted of literate, autonomous, critical, constructive people, capable of translating ideas into action, individually or collectively – the world would change. (J. Galtung, *from his remarks at the International Symposium for Literacy, Persepolis, Iran, 1975*)

For almost 1 billion adults in the world today, adult literacy has to be the first step toward education. They have been bypassed by the school system; they can not read or write.

Knowledge in the oral cultures of the world is helping them survive, but it is mere survival. More knowledge is needed, and most of this knowledge is locked in the printed page.

Before taking leave, let us look more carefully at the literacy/illiteracy situation in today's world. What hope is there that we will have universal literacy in our times? What role can we as ordinary citizens play in literacy promotion?

A STATUS REPORT ON LITERACY

As I was writing this practical guide, I read the following news item in the local newspaper.

Illiteracy has declined worldwide for the first time, a United Nations report says.

The United Nations Educational, Scientific and Cultural Organization said the number of illiterate people in 1990 was 948 million, 2 million fewer than in 1985. A further decline to 935 million is expected by the end of the century, the report says.

The number of illiterate people had risen from 890 million in 1970 with rapid growth in the underdeveloped nations. The report said 98 per cent of illiteracy is found in poverty-stricken Third World nations, and the majority of the illiterate are women.

The report is expected to be submitted Tuesday to the fifty-one member Executive Board of the Paris-based agency, which is reviewing the results of the United Nations' International Literacy Year 1990.

'Encouraging as these statistics may be as proof that illiteracy can be vanquished, the progress they document is painfully slow', the report said.

The percentage of adult illiterates has declined from about 38.5 in 1970 to 26.6 in 1990, and will be reduced to 21.8 by the year 2000.

About 27 million American are functionally illiterate, according to the United States Department of Education.

According to UNESCO figures, the highest rate of adult illiteracy is in Africa at 54 per cent, followed by Asia, 36 per cent, and Latin America, 17 per cent.

A CATALOGUE OF HOPES

Our hopes for the universalization of literacy are high. Our hopes and realities do not match. It was hoped that with the end of the cold war, resources wasted in preparations for war would become available for works of peace. Universal literacy was always on the list of works of peace. These hopes have been shattered.

UNESCO has been talking about 'Education for All' by the year 2000. That is barely six years away. 'Education for All' means primary education for all children – boys and girls, everywhere in the world. It also means literacy for all the world's youth and adults – men and women.

One can question the practicality of the above but not its inspirational value.

The World Conference on Education for All held in Jomtien, Thailand during March 5–9, 1990 established the more realistic targets listed below.

- *Primary education*: Each country will strive to ensure that at least 80 per cent of all 14-year-old boys and girls attain a common level of learning achievement for primary education, set by the respective national authorities.

- *Adult education*: Access to basic skills and knowledge for all.

- *Literacy*: Massive reduction of illiteracy with targets to be set by each country prioritized by age and sex.

POSSIBILITIES WITHIN CONSTRAINTS

We cannot play God to stop all wars to have permanent peace. We cannot banish racism and prejudice to establish a common human brotherhood. We cannot wish away greed and selfishness that we may be able to do something about real hunger and deprivation. We cannot by a simple wish make education and literacy central to our lives everywhere.

But there are possibilities even within the constraints of the present world. Initiatives are in our individual hands.

A BOOK FOR PRACTITIONERS

I was asked to write a practical guide for functional literacy workers. I took it to mean the following: First, that I should write this guide from the point of view of practitioners, particularly teachers and supervisors. Second, that I should include and discuss ideas and practices that are directly usable in daily practice. Third, that my language should be clear and understandable.

PRACTITIONERS IN MY MIND'S EYE

I have tried to do all this to the best of my ability. In all I have written here, I have kept literacy teachers and supervisors in my mind's eye. I was always thinking of real literacy teachers and supervisors that I had met in India, in Afghanistan, the Islamic Republic of Iran, the United Republic of Tanzania, Malawi, Botswana, Zimbabwe, Bolivia and elsewhere. I have tried to anticipate their questions and concerns, and answer those concerns to the best of my ability.

In doing so, I have tried not to under-estimate the intelligence of my readers. I have, therefore, not merely talked of 'how-to-do' but also of 'why' to do what is suggested and why to do it in a particular way. At the same time, I have tried not to over-estimate the knowledge and experience of my readers. Some of my explanations, therefore, may begin to sound too elaborate.

Doing functional literacy is a bit more than common sense. It is somewhat technical. It has not been possible, therefore, to avoid all technical words. Wherever possible, explanations of these technical words have been provided. Those who read this book in vernacular translations may have less of a problem here than those who read it in English or French.

NOBODY READS THE SAME BOOK

It is often said that nobody reads the same book. This means that people read a book in terms of their own experience. Those who already have considerable experience get more from a book. Again, people with different experiences get somewhat different things from the same book.

Furthermore, books become more useful when read more than once. Read this guide as you begin your work on a functional literacy project, but come back to it and read it again after you have finished one or two cycles of literacy work.

You may also find it quite useful to develop a peer group of literacy teachers to read and discuss the book together.

We have talked quite a bit about what this practical guide was going to be. Now that you have read it, you should be able to make a judgement on if we succeeded. You can judge as to how far we did succeed, if we did not succeed fully.

We will be happy to hear from you. Please let us know what you think of the practical guide, how might we improve it for a possible second edition.

Bibliography

Bhola, H.S. (1979) *Curriculum Development for Functional Literacy and Nonformal Education Programs*. Bonn: DSE.

Bhola, H.S. (198) *Program and Curriculum Development in the Post-literacy Stages*. Bonn: DSE.

Bhola, H.S. (1984) *Campaigning for Literacy: Eight National Experiences of the Twentieth Century, with a Memorandum to Decision-Makers*. Paris: UNESCO.

Bhola, H.S. (1988) *World Trends and Issues in Adult Education*. London/Paris: Jessica Kingsley.

Bhola, H.S. (1990) *Evaluating 'Literacy for Development' Projects, Programs and Campaigns. Evaluation Planning, Design and Implementation, and Utilization of Evaluation Results*. Hamburg/Bonn: UIE/DSE.

Bhola, H.S., Bhola, J.K. (1984) *Planning and Organization of Literacy Campaigns, Programs and Projects*. Bonn: DSE.

Bishop, A.J. (1988) Mathematics Education in its Cultural Context. *Educational Studies in Mathematics 19*, No. 2, 179–91.

Giere, U., Ouane, A., Ranaweera, A. and M. (1990) L'Alphabétisation dans les Pays en Développement: Bibliographie Analytique. *Bulletin du Bureau International d'Éducation/Bulletin of the International Bureau of Education*, No. 254/257, JanuaryDecember. (Prepared for the International Bureau of Education (IBE) by the UNESCO Institute of Education (UIE).)

Gray, W.S. (1969) *The Teaching of Reading and Writing. An International Survey*. (2nd ed.) Paris: UNESCO.

Malawi Government. Ministry of Community Services. (1991) *Training Manual for Trainers of Functional Literacy Instructors*. Lilongwe: National Centre for Literacy and Adult Education.

Marshall, J., Chigarire, D., Francisco, H., Goncalves, A., and Nhantumbo, L. *Training for Empowerment: A Kit for Materials for Popular Literacy Workers Based on an Exchange among Educators from Mozambique, Nicaragua and Brazil*. Toronto: International Council for Adult Education, n.d.

Ouane, A., Armengol, Mercy Abreu de, and Sharma, D.V. (1990) *Handbook on Training for Post-literacy and Basic Education*. Hamburg: UIE.

Rassekh, S. (1991) *Perspectives on Literacy: A Selected World Bibliography*. Paris: UNESCOIBE.

Singh, S. (1976) *Learning to Read and Reading to Learn: An Approach to a System of Literacy Instruction.* Amersham/Tehran: Hulton Educational Publications/International Institute for Adult Literacy Methods.

UNESCO. (1981) *Literacy Curriculum and Materials Development. Portfolio of Literacy Materials. Series I: Four Monographs.* No. 1: *Curriculum Development in Literacy,* 73 pp. No. 2: *Motivational Materials Development,* 54 pp. No. 3: *Instructional Materials Development,* 92 pp. No. 4: *Follow-up Materials Development,* 59 pp. Bangkok: UNESCO/ROEAP.

UNESCO. (1982) *Planning, Administration and Monitoring in Literacy. Portfolio of Literacy Materials. Monograph Series. Series 2.* No. 1: *Planning of Literacy Programmes,* 18 pp. No. 2: *Administration of Literacy Programmes,* 16 pp. No. 3: *Monitoring of Literacy Programmes,* 66 pp. Bangkok: UNESCO/ROEAP.

Vélis, Jean-Pierre. (1990) *Through a Glass, Darkly. Functional Illiteracy in Industrialized Countries.* Paris: UNESCO.